FIVE SHEETS OF PLYWOOD:

A PRACTICAL GUIDE FOR STARTING YOUR OWN BUSINESS

Written by

SPIROS G. RAFTIS

ISBN: 1-4107-4571-6 (e-book)
ISBN: 1-4107-4574-0 (Paperback)
ISBN: 1-4107-4570-8 (Hardcover)

This book is printed on acid free paper.

1stBooks - rev. 05/22/03

I have often wondered about the value of a page in a book where the author gives credit to those he thinks helped him develop his written project. I thought the page was a nice gesture. I know now the acknowledgement page defines the realization of the author's humility. I wonder no longer for I admit writing FIVE SHEETS OF PLYWOOD humbled me.

I wish to thank my wife Anastasia for her unwavering faith in my dream and me; I know the sacrifices she made to push me on.

I thank my sons George, Chris, and my daughter Cynthia for their contributions to my life, and to their growing impact on the legacy of the Raftis' family.

FORWARD

THE UNITED STATES OF AMERICA QUARANTEES EACH CITIZEN THE RIGHT TO DEVELOP WHATEVER TALENTS, GIFTS, BLESSINGS OR RESOURCES TO THE BEST OF THEIR ABILITIES.

GOD BLESS AMERICA

OTHER NATIONS OF THE WORLD DO NOT OFFER THESE CHOICES AND OPPORTUNITIES.

I had a good paying career, and a growing sense of security. My employer sold me shares of stock in his firm. At age 26, three years out of college, here I was a successful salesman and part owner of the company, and then out on the street. Fired! WOW!

Where is the justice in this world? What a blow; I slowly picked up the pieces. I decided starting my own business was the only way to prevent being ripped off again.

Owning your own business also gives a person the opportunity of earning the maximum return in proportion to one's abilities. The book, **FIVE SHEETS OF PLYWOOD,** is a <u>must</u> <u>buy</u> guidebook if one plans on starting a business; it will help in building a successful business, and grant a maximum return on the abilities invested.

Many of the messages, lessons, and reflections are of unexpected experiences anyone might encounter while building a business, for example:

>PARTNERS—Outline Divorce Papers First
>BARE ESSENTIALS OF SUBSISTENCE, and why that
>   is important
>LAWYERS—BANKERS
>UNIONS—I was first hit with two employees, and then
>   thirteen
>DETERMINATION—how important it is—LESSON 13

FIVE SHEETS OF PLYWOOD gives advice from the trenches—shirtsleeve advice. Even if only one piece of advice shines through, it may be the difference between failure and success.

I asked a friend of mine who just started a business to review the book, she replied, "Spiros, the part that impressed me was somewhere you said I could always go get a job. The thought helped me to quit worrying, and pay full attention to my toy business."

Much is written in this book about will power, fortitude, character, and catharsis of hang-ups (LESSON 26.) If you start your own business you will conclude not enough was written.

Here the story tells of a fourteen-year-old kid mopping floors, and then at age twenty-six takes five sheets of plywood, (MESSAGE # 5,) AND BUILDS A MULTI-MILLION DOLLAR EMPIRE— EMPLOYING OVER 200 PEOPLE—WHO HAS DESIGNED AND HOLDS 28 PATENTS FOR VALVES USED ON ENVIRONMENTAL AND STORM WATER APPLICATIONS, AND WHO HAS TRAVELED THE WORLD OVER. A kid who took advantage of the opportunity AMERICA offers everyone.

FIVE SHEETS OF PLYWOOD is divided into five parts: "THE NEED," THE USE," "THE VALUE," "A CONSULTANT'S BRIEF GUIDELINE ON SUCCESSION PLANNING," and "START-UP ACCOUNTING AND FINANCE GUIDE.

Regardless if you are one of the readers who is just starting a business, or the one well into the journey, or perhaps, the one planning for succession, what ever the stage of growth "THE NEED" section intends to shake, rattle, and roll the person to a finer appreciation of the birthright America offers to all. This section sells the need for self-confidence, faith and hope. The messages show what level of success can be achieved by unleashing the power of positive attitude as positive thinking serves to trigger that kind of attitude.

The section entitled THE USE contains lessons I learned working a plan to achieve the goals of where I wanted to be. The section is intentionally structured to appear in the middle of the book, ties together the beliefs, values, attitudes and goals that equal the ideology of success permeated throughout **FIVE SHEETS OF PLYWOOD.**

The third section must be called THE VALUE for this part stresses the journey that if done right never ends. A business morphs into new and different shapes constantly, as it struggles to satisfy changing needs uses and values. Different problems rise up needing not-thought-of-yet-solutions. Management, work force, sales staff—not even dreamed of in the beginning—create opportunities if only someone thought of these variables as such. The bottom line—the last line—of section three ends with what it is feels like passing on a successful business as a legacy to family members.

Part IV delves into the troublesome problem of "Succession Planning." John Ward and Craig Arnoff, two professional consultants, developed the excerpt that spells out the main problems and solutions when it comes time to change leadership. Turning over a business to the second generation is like starting a new business. I went through all this, and believe when I say it was painful—that is why the section was included.

PART V develops a model START-UP ACCOUNTING AND FINANCE GUIDE, by CFO, Mr. Joe Myers. I asked my CFO if he met a person who is starting his or her business what would you advise? What would the do's and don'ts be? His reply in this section is solid, good, and helpful guide to financing.

FIVE SHEETS OF PLYWOOD, is one of those must buy guidebooks that will, hopefully, lead you to a successful business. Just keep in mind nothing will come with ease, but everything comes to those willing to go after it and stay with it. Success is a masterful recipe consisting of several powerful ingredients such as will power, fortitude, perseverance, and inner belief in one's self. If you have those ingredients, simply let them rise to success.

GO FOR IT!

TABLE OF CONTENTS

PART I

THE NEED

Message # 1
Reality of the Business World - Why I Started a Business

I WAS FIRED!

After graduation from college, I went to work for a manufacturer's agent who represented ten different valve companies. Learning details and features about various styles of valves certainly proved to be an enormous education and gigantic challenge. There were a lot of new things my brain had to consume.

Luckily, I was assigned a virgin, undeveloped sales territory, which was a rather large undertaking, but gave me the chance to conquer, develop self-confidence, and to become that successful industrial salesman. I attacked the job with a pioneer spirit.

Wanting to establish this new sales territory, I worked like a demon. I studied it thoroughly. I came to know what plants were in my territory, where they were located, and the principle buyers. I began to make record-building sales, which not only created substantial profit for my bank account, but it also developed my self-confidence, my ego, and pride.

The owner of the company was impressed with my drive, work ethic, and progress, informing me that his company had a stock purchase plan, and I was eligible to become a stockholder. This was an excellent opportunity to become an owner, the dream of a lifetime, at such an early age, an opportunity that truly would reward my abilities. I was already earning commissions beyond my comprehension so why not become an owner? I was flying high. Nothing could stop me now! I would not stop until I reached the top.

POW! Three years later, the owner called me into his office.

I thought on the way in, *I wonder what size bonus the boss is going to give me.*

He told me my percentage of commission was too high and would have to be reduced. I was receiving sixty percent of the commission, with the remaining forty percent going to the company. He laid it out for me, "We will have to change your contract and lower the rate to fifty-fifty."

2

No bonus. I was supposed to take a pay <u>cut</u>.

"Now, you know that isn't fair! We have a contract and I'm sure you'd like to do the right thing, and keep your word per that contract."

"Things were different when I hired you." His face looked downward.

I hate it when people cannot look me in the eye when speaking directly to me. It gives me the impression that they are either lying, or have bad news.

I answered in rebuttal. "No, <u>you</u> weren't getting any sales from my territory at that time. You should stick to your contract. Why didn't you make the contract fifty-fifty at the time we signed the agreement?"

No answer.

I continued. "Look, you're a good businessman. Can't we work this out and be fair? I mean you are making a lot of money, and not just from my sales. You should live up to our agreement, keep your word!" He winced, and then ignored me by looking elsewhere.

I pushed on, for as long as I was speaking, I thought, I was in control. "You expect me to be the most knowledgeable, debonair, successful salesman on the road, and the dumbest about my pay?"

He looked up at me and smiled. "Spiros, it's great to be single. Think about taking that cut."

I was in a state of shock hearing his proposal. I had assumed he would come to his senses, realizing my value to the company. I had assumed I could convince him of the errors of his ways by sound logic and reason. I knew I was right. He dismissed me and I stormed out of his office.

Some time went by with me seething at every passing moment.

I was again called into the owner's office, only to participate in a brief, to-the-point conversation that took all of twenty seconds. He informed me my commission, for the betterment of the company, was <u>definitely</u> to be cut in half!

"That's ridiculous!

There would be no slicing of <u>my</u> earnings at any time. I should be getting a raise instead. After all, I'm one of the best salesmen on the staff; I brought in big orders. The company should be within that proverbial profit margin on my new customer's alone. Why should I give up what is truly mine? I do the legwork, and take time to convince these customers that my corporation would only give them the best in workmanship, performance, and support service.

I was firm when I answered back, "No, I would not take a commission cut. I am not going to give up what I worked so hard to achieve. I am not going to give up what is rightfully mine."

He was quick answering back, "You are fired."

It took less than a second for him to say it, "You are fired." Instead of moving up to the top, I was headed out the door to oblivion. What an ungrateful SOB. Didn't I have every right to be angry?

The company then took my territory and divided it between two people whom they paid each a fifty-fifty commission split. Here I was 26, a salesman/stockholder of renown being replaced by not one, but two other salesmen, working the territory that I had breathed the first breadth of economic life.

Now, 26, I was unemployed. I know I wasn't the only person this happened to, but at the time, it was quite a blow to my existence, my rather enlarged ego. I found myself somewhat unstable and insecure, believing nothing was permanent in this business world if they can get away with firing a good salesman, a stockholder, and an owner!

I pouted for two weeks, but did not let resentment get the best of me. I took time to review my qualifications realizing I had learned a great deal. I was successful in selling industrial products to large corporations, and small businesses. That was worth a lot.

Because of my degree in engineering, I understood and could point out various technical features of any other type of valves within the marketplace. I had traveled through all of Western Pennsylvania and West Virginia, knew where plants were located, personal names, positions, purchasing agents, plant maintenance people, and their managers. I could be a manufacturer representative MYSELF!

People often go into business because they were fired, or their company relocated, or there was a reduction in force.

When fired, individuals have a tendency to start with an underlying build-up of resentment.

One morning I awoke to a sudden realization that there really was a bright and positive side to my particular circumstance. Yes, I could "cut the mustard," and start a business if I applied myself.

Smart folks find out pouting does not help. They must appraise their plus/minus situation, deciding their course of action.

A friend of mine told me the following story at the time:

Nelson was a shell-shocked World War I veteran who came home from the battlefield and refused to accept a disability pension. He refused such a benefit, stating, 'I fought as a patriotic citizen of the United States. I love my country and wanted to fight for its freedom and won't accept a disability check."

The government, in an effort to help him financially, worked up a plan with local officials and actually made this veteran believe his disability check was a work paycheck. The mayor of the town gave him the job of polishing the cannon and cannon ball outside the courthouse. Every time his disability pension contained a raise, he was told the increase was because of his hard work.

One afternoon he went to the mayor's office, throwing down both polish and rags while making a rather unexpected declaration. "I'm downright tired of polishing someone else's cannon and cannon ball. I quit and with the money I've saved, I'll buy a cannon and cannon ball, and go into business for myself."

If you recently got laid off, or fired, like Nelson, take inventory of the skills, knowledge acquired, and take advantage of your assets.

In most cases, a person starting a business does not anticipate the move, does not give himself or herself ample time to prepare, or plan for it, except in the case of the shell-shocked veteran.

I concluded that the only way to prevent being ripped-off again was to start my own business. I refused to allow myself to be lied to and betrayed again. My resolve to succeed strengthened each time I remembered standing in that office watching someone who controlled my future look elsewhere in the room as he contemplated his next move, which was to fire me. I had turned seething resentment into positive resolve.

Self-pity would only make me a victim. My life's dream had nothing to do with being a victim.

Message # 2
No Money

I had next to no money, was fired without notice, did not have time to plan and prepare for a new venture, was mixed up in my thinking at the beginning, and demoralized for I was uncertain of my future.

My first endeavor for several years was to become a manufacturer representative – a business I knew. In looking for companies to sell for and products, I saw an opportunity to manufacture my own valves – "A RUBBER PINCH VALVE." This started me on a quest to becoming a valve manufacturer.

I did have ambition, self-confidence, and a burning desire. I designed a new style valve that I felt had many features over what was available in the market. I felt so strongly about it I decided this would be my "new business." I had to work with a bare minimum of essentials with what little money I had. No need for office furniture. No need for a secretary. No need for actual office space. No need for a toilet (more about that later).

A properly displayed catalog for sales purposes was necessary so customers could learn all about my valve, which I applied for patents. I needed to get my message out to clients/corporations.

Nothing else regarding the set-up of my business was as important as that catalog which had to point out the advantages of my product through pictures and explanatory text.

It was necessary to sell my products by describing my product and showing them my catalog, and explaining how my valve would benefit their business, their profit.

A customer in Kingsport, Tennessee, who saw and read my catalog, determined the advantages, read the benefits, and thought he should purchase my valves. This customer assumed without a doubt in his mind that I had an office and shop, that I was a manufacturer. I survived during those beginning days all because I printed a great looking catalog.

Message # 3
How I Bought the Land

There is no sure-fire way of starting a business. There just aren't courses of study that can guarantee you success or show you each step of the way into a world of immediate profit for your new endeavor. You will not see 'Starting a Business-101' within the list of college courses offered anywhere.

NOT HAVING MONEY IS A BASIC PROBLEM INVOLVING THOSE WHO HAVE FINALLY DECIDED TO GO AHEAD WITH THEIR DREAMS AND HOPES FOR THE FUTURE BY PLUNGING INTO OWNERSHIP OF THEIR OWN BUSINESS.

I needed a manufacturing plant. I sought out the expertise of a real estate agent. After explaining my situation, he began showing me rental properties within low-rent districts such as storefronts, old foundries with dirt floors, old garages; you name it, he showed it. The prices were all in the same range—between $400.00-$900.00 per month.

"I can't afford it!" I yelled. "The idea is to make a profit not go in debt! I'd have to spend a fortune remodeling those old dumps into what I actually need." Yes, all were definitely out of my monetary range. After several weeks of this here-and-there shop looking, the real estate agent came up with a possible solution.

"Look, I know you're tight for cash. I have a parcel of undeveloped ground for sale, almost sixty acres. It's located in the suburbs, and I will sell you an acre. My asking price is $2,000 an acre."

"How come so low?"

"If you bought the property and began manufacturing, the utility companies would bring up power, water, and gas lines, opening up the rest of the property for me."

"I get the picture…if you sell to me at $2,000 an acre and utilities are set up, you could profit more from sales of the remaining acreage?"

"Yup! I'd say I would have no problem doubling, even tripling the acreage price for the balance of land. This is a good location."

7

"Sold! Now, about paying for it."

"Well, how did you intend to pay in the first place? This isn't going to be a problem, is it?"

"I hope not. Anyway, I had in mind paying about $50.00 a month for the first year and $100.00 thereafter until the property is paid off. You see, this is all I've got, actually it's all I can afford."

"Mister, you've got to be kidding, right?"

"No, sir. I'm not. I have to buy concrete blocks and other building supplies. I have to work part-time jobs just to pay for this venture."

"Boy, you are tough—full of drive but no money."

"Hey, you will be saving income tax money since payment of the lot would be carried for several years, and your capital gains could be spread over two years."

I kept explaining why I needed the land for the next twenty minutes. I emphasized how my lifetime ambition lay in this piece of ground. I talked so long; he succumbed and took the offer. He probably agreed to shut me up, and also to get the ball rolling on his property; it had been for sale for over a year.

A few days later he confirmed my offer. "Congratulations, Spiros. You are now a land owner." He shook my hand as I proudly came to that realization myself.

"That's right! I am fortunate! Someday this property will house a huge company as my business and I grow together."

"I'll just bet you'll make it to success some day. Good luck."

"Thanks."

"If you need me again…and I'm sure you might, just call. You have my card, right?"

"You bet I will." It was a warm feeling to suddenly say to myself 'I am a land owner of land for a manufacturing plant.' The successful key to this real estate transaction was that I never at any time gave in to embarrassment at what little money I had to offer, nor was I afraid to ask for exactly what I wanted. I maintained an air of self-confidence and sincerity without any hesitation. You need that attitude to come across with *any* business deal. After all, it was my money, my future, and it will be your money, your future, too!

I could now proceed to build my office and plant. The process would take time, but I was certain of its completion because I had the required drive, strength, attitude, and mental outlook to do it, no matter how long it took.

There are two reasons I wanted to tell you this story. The first is that now looking back on this situation I am amazed that I actually pulled that whole deal off—no money down, $50.00 a month. Secondly, to point out that America is such a huge country within itself, there still remains much unsold, low-cost property waiting to be purchased.

Somewhere there is somebody looking to sell, either for tax purposes or other reasons. Location of property may vary from suburbia, to a rural country area, or perhaps in a desert, but it's available.

Message # 4
FIVE SHEETS OF PLYWOOD

I had the land. I needed an instant office.

Thus came my five sheets of plywood office, I nailed together four sheets of 3/4"x 4x 8' plywood for the walls, and used the fifth sheet as a roof. That is what it took to build my first office. That was all I could afford.

IMPOSSIBLE YOU MIGHT SAY. DO NOT LAUGH IT WAS FOR REAL!

I cut out a door, attached the front door with the cellar door hinges, and installed padlock hardware on the door.

I cut three feet from the fifth sheet, (the remainder ended up as the roof,) and made it a desk, using a chair I brought from home. Next came the installation of a phone and I was in business.

Bare essentials of subsistence! A term I carried in my "psyche" for the next sixteen months, also serving, as one of my key to success.

Don't think being fired did not affect me because it did. The experience was, indeed, extremely traumatic for me because I had worked so hard to obtain those orders, as well as become a part owner. Rejection damages one's ego, and is difficult to explain. It took a lot of serious thought before I actually overcame this incident.

The fact of the matter is, I did overcome, and learned a valuable lesson: IT IS NOT THE EVENTS IN ONE'S LIFE THAT DETERMINES WHO WE ARE, IT IS HOW WE REACT TO THOSE EVENTS THAT MAKES US WHO WE REALLY ARE.

I worked out of this four-foot-by four-foot, eight-foot-high enclosure for seven months. The only thing that actually got me was—THE LONELINESS.

I felt like a monk praying within his small living quarters in the monastery, or a priest waiting to hear confessions in a confessional cubicle. No happy hour, no martini lunches, no companionship for that debonair, industrial salesman…who now had his own office with nary an inch for so much as a file cabinet, but, instead, a cardboard box to store papers. The dirt floor was definitely cold, but no time to worry about that. I wore warm stockings, clothes and shoes. I did not care about simple, minor adjustments. I had an office now!

Incidentally, <u>I chose to get married to a woman named Anastasia, during this time who knew my position</u>, and was willing assist me in any way necessary.

My son, to this day, shakes his head in disbelief that this small-shed building, resembling an outhouse, was my office for seven months. I had no toilet facilities except for toilet paper and the wild woods surrounding my land. I lived like this for seven months but remained cheerful and determined. Are you *really* determined? Do you have self-confidence? Could you do something similar to this if you had to? If your answer is yes, you are ready to begin your own business. Go down to **Home Depot™** and get started.

As I reflect back now a used office trailer would have solved my problem better. Who knew? Being determined has its compensation; <u>I was my own boss.</u>

Pittsburgh, Pennsylvania is a beautiful touch of nature in the summer, but during the winter months, forests appear bland, cold, and almost dead to the view.

The dirt road leading to my "office" was on a twenty-five degree slope. There was very little grass. Rain contributed to a multitude of deep, mud ruts in the road. No matter how hard I tried, this mud around my office would somehow end up all over our home.

Anastasia had her transition—a husband, a college graduate, and an engineer no less-coming home with a lunch bucket, mud in cuffs of my trousers, and tracking mud all over the house.

"My goodness, Spiros! You're soaked with mud from head to toe. You'll catch your death of cold!" She would help me off with my coat, having supper ready, and serve it all with a hot, relaxing cup of tea.

"Sorry about the mud. The weather doesn't want to cooperate…"

She quickly interrupted, "Just be careful driving in that winter weather up that dirt road. Stay as warm as you can, don't catch pneumonia. That's all I'm worried about! I do not want to lose you."

That was my wife back then. God bless her patience, cooperation, moral support, and thrift, all without complaint. Anastasia was and is very much a part of my success story.

We lived for two years in a six-room house. The only furniture was in the kitchen and bedroom. The BARE ESSENTIALS OF SUBSISTENCE even in my married life. My wife experienced the very meaning of that phrase right along with me.

The best tip I can provide at this point in the book is to have a serious one-on-one talk with your spouse, spouse-to-be, *before* attempting to start your own business. You will need his/her support many times over and probably for the duration of your married life.

She cannot be buying new dresses. BARE ESSENTIALS OF SUBSISTENCE.

I'm reminded of a person I hired for sales. He loved the product, territory, incentive, and bonus challenge. He quit after two weeks. His wife did not want him to stay away from home over night. Business trips sometimes require several days of meetings.

Make certain your spouse is willing to go along with you on every phase of the road. There will be both good and bad times, seemingly more of the bad experiences at the beginning. Getting started takes money, and time away from a marriage.

He/she must be willing to help sacrifice time and energy. Think of the future, when profit begins to make an appearance, little by little; it is then that he/she can enjoy the fruits of sacrifices made. It will definitely come.

Do not deal with a spouse or live-in who is not willing to make sacrifices or give of their time; you're better off getting a job. Spouses are very important in marriage, but more important when your business becomes involved in your relationship.

Message # 5
Fear of Failure

Mental attitude has a large bearing on success or failure.

Three simple but immensely powerful thoughts guide our every action or inaction from birth: 1) fear of failure, 2) fear of rejection, and 3) fear of punishment. "NO!" The word is the verbal expression we associate with those fears, the trigger that releases a lifetime of collected impressions. "NO" came before we were made to stand in the corner, ordered to bed or spanked by an angry hand. This hand generally belonged to someone who loved us but also had the strong belief, as did their parents, a child should be seen and not heard, doing only what he/she was told. Our parents and teachers were instructing us to have respect for others (particularly elders) as well as a proper regard for other people' property as well as your own. It did not exactly teach us self-respect. That had to come as we became older, which was difficult.

"NO!" came before someone turned his or her back on us. "NO!" along with our reaction to inner fears build into the basis for ideas of good bad, right, or wrong. "NO!" Don't do that; "NO! Stop that, or "NO! You'll get burned. "NO!" is leveled in both judgment and punishment. We learn "NO!" Bad boy! And we are taught its opposite as well..."YES!" Good boy! "YES!" Good girl!

We are graded on levels. In school there is a level of good and bad ranging from A to F, but it only serves to enhance the ides of being judged by others, of seeking approval. The fear of disapproval, the fear of failure, the fear of rejection, the fear of punishment, the fear of hearing, and "NO!" <u>all undermine our ability to decide and learn for our success</u>. Fear closes us off from ourselves by turning us outward, looking without instead of within for approval, for fulfillment, or for value. We need to form our own self-approval, our own inner self-confidence, thereby enabling us to affirmatively, without hesitation, say: "<u>GO FOR IT!</u>"

Hopefully, you are over the "NO!" as well as the "Fear of Failure" syndromes.

SPIROS G. RAFTIS

Self-confidence is your ONLY diving force. You'd better have it or you're not ready with what it takes for the responsibility of starting your own business. Repeat the "I CAN DO IT" syndrome phrase daily...and actually try to convince yourself to BELIEVE it! You will need this power of positive attitude to avoid or properly deal with any possible hang-ups.

Message # 6
Go For It

People have asked for my opinion many times regarding going into business for themselves. I generally begin by telling them that if it is something they have always wanted to do, I answer quite freely, "Go for it! If you don't make it, at least you gave it your best try and got it out of your system."

Look at it this way—when you are in your deathbed, you can say 'I tried and died'.

Will Rogers once said, "You have to go out on a limb, that is where the fruit is."

If the business venture does not work out for you, you can always get a real (this word might hurt when you say it after failing in your own business) 'JOB'. Some would say getting a job is a piece of cake. It all depends on whether or not the cake has icing (benefits, good wages, vacations, hospitalization, etc.)

There has been a trend in this country the last twenty years for people to start their own business. The reason for this prevailing tendency is that most corporations have become very complex, no longer offering job longevity. Workers are simply sick and tired of working for 'Slave Drivers', (CEO's who expect their employees to do a multitude of tasks for two persons…and then some…just for a single salary.)

I have an acquaintance with a Bachelor's Degree in Business Administration. She had recently been laid off from a rather well known steel firm, accepting a new position with a local lumber supply company. As an administrative assistant she was expected to answer the phones, do the bookkeeping consisting of accounts payable/receivable/payroll, take dictation and perform other secretarial work, sort the mail, and wait on customers. At the end of one day, she could only wonder when they were going to ask her to scrub walls and clean the commodes.

Several disappointing attempts later, after working (actually slaving) long hours for other employers, she finally took my advice, and eventually began a worthwhile project. It was something she really felt compelled to do…own and operate a personnel agency in an effort to help others secure DECENT employment from legitimate local corporations and small business firms. She carefully tested and went over not only each employee's qualifications and references, but also checked out future employer's complete job descriptions/wages as well. Her firm is now one of the leading employment agencies in the country.

Companies who merge give the impression that their jobs are safe and secure. When you hear the word MERGE and the phrase, 'all will go well and be prosperous for employees', do not believe it. Mergers, from past figures and facts, most generally squeeze employees right out of their jobs, CEO's work and plan more for stock options, than the growth of any given corporation or the welfare of employees.

When having a bad day while running your own business, think of the old alternate direction in which you would have to return…you could once again be working for someone else, making you <u>twice</u> as miserable as ever. Just think about that for a while and remember this. When you begin your own business, going backwards is not an option, 'Tis forward and onward with nary a failure.' Perhaps there will be a wrong decision or two, but these must be treated as mistakes to be corrected. Failures please do not think this way, not now, not ever.

Message # 7
Know Thyself—Your Hang-ups

KNOW THYSELF

Up until ninth grade in high school, I had hang-ups accompanied by a negative attitude. My grades were D or below. As a matter of fact, for the longest time in elementary school through to ninth grade, I was known as the class clown. I thought I had everything figured out pertaining to my life. When I dropped out or graduated from high school, whichever came first, I would get a job cleaning buildings or doing maintenance of some sort. If I work very hard maybe I'll become a building superintendent of sorts.

Then one night a friend of my father's entered my life. He tutored English to Turkish students in Pittsburgh studying metallurgy at the University of Pittsburgh.

"Make something of yourself", he said to me. "You're not like your father, an immigrant with no schooling. You should be ashamed of yourself loafing in school and getting such lousy grades! You live here in Pittsburgh—the largest steel town in the world." He paused while checking over the grades on my report card, which he asked to see. He merely shook his head in a negative manner.

"Young men from Turkey come to America to study metallurgy. I teach them English and these students believe themselves to be the luckiest people on earth. They are studying in America and totally believe in what America has to offer them as students. You live here, born and raised here. Wise up, young man! You can do much better." His deep voice echoed liked thunder in my ears.

All I can say now is it wasn't easy to work, to attend classes, to catch up. I found out it is not true in America that only rich people attend college. I wasn't rich but, by changing course, and with hard work and perseverance, I graduated from the University of Pittsburgh with a Metallurgical Engineering degree. This proves that any one who really wants to accomplish whatever he/she sets out to do can do it.

I ask that you take time now to review your hang-ups (we all have a few.) File them away where they cannot hurt anymore. Give yourself a complete purging of mind and matter, a catharsis so to speak. Plan to make something of yourself. There is no place to go but forward into the boundaries of your own dream world, which will turn out to be your very own lucrative, profitable business.

Keep that positive attitude and believe "I CAN DO IT," believe even after you reach your ultimate goal, which should be no less than complete success!

Message # 8
Mopping Floors

MOPPING FLOORS

I write this book not to inflate my ego, but rather to point out that I overcame these adversities, and to forewarn you that adversities are coming your way.

My father was a sexton of our church, which definitely placed me on the bottom of both the economic and social ladders. We were 'poor as church mice', as the old saying goes.

He had been employed by Bell Telephone as a building superintendent at one of the exchanges. He got laid off in the middle of the depression. The only job he could find was as a sexton of our Church. With a wife and two children, he accepted it and got stuck there.

From the age of twelve to eighteen, I helped by continuously mopping floors as required (Saturdays and other times after school) not only the church, but the community center as well. Seemed the only time I got to rest while working was when it came time to polish various receptacles and serving utensils at the church, being allowed to sit at a large table while enhancing the appearance of all brass and silver.

My father paid me one dollar for an entire day's work. This was all he could afford. He needed help, thus enabling him to complete electrical work, painting, plumbing, candle making, and other church chores. He wanted to teach me all of these trades. What I think now, for he never said this, he really wanted to spend time with me, and give me the facts of life and society. I failed to fully appreciate his guidance during this time nor did I realize back then that it was more valuable than all the trades he taught me.

Later on, I realized this was the larger benefit that we worked together and he shared his words of wisdom. In turn, I now share those words with my siblings.

There was no time permitted for baseball, basketball, tennis, and bike riding, no playtime at all. Time could not be wasted on such simple things such as sports or fun time. Those particular teen years in

19

my life allotted nothing in the way of pleasures or fun as athletic participation had no meaning or value, serving no purpose in his eyes. It teaches nothing (per my parents' point of view).

Occasionally, I would walk back into the church interior open the door, and cry out LOUD AND CLEAR, "God, cut me a break!" That was my prayer.

At times I visualized myself at the bottom of a fifty-five-gallon drum, reaching up to the rim with a hope I could pull myself up and out, into something better.

As explained earlier, a friend of the family lit one candle. I had to overcome social as well as economic depression.

There are many, many people in America who probably can tell you similar stories of early, endured hardships, and visualize them selves as I did, curled up in the bottom of a 55-gallon-drum. Like myself, they made every effort to overcome each barrier, becoming successful in one way or another, turning a penniless situation towards some money and then on to big money.

Make up your mind what you want to do. I never had enough money for anything much less enough to begin my own business! But here I am today…a millionaire.

Get rid of self-pity for you do not have to mop floors the rest of your life.

Message # 9
The Luck of the Irish

As a teenager, I was brainwashed by friends. I heard it so often that I actually began to believe it. "Spiros, you are Greek, they will never hire you for any big position. You'll be lucky you can find a laborer's job."

At age 43, I told an Irish friend of mine (incidentally, he was an executive) how tough I had it at that time, and how lucky he was to be Irish instead of Greek.

"You have it made because you're Irish and part of the White-Anglo-Saxon - Protestant Society".

"Hey, where in the hell did you grow up?" he asked. "You think Irish people have it easy, huh? Do you know that the English hate the Irish?

"They do? They are?"

"Yes, and that isn't the half of it! There was the potato famine..."

He then recounted all the dastardly deeds done to the Irish that I, thinking narrow-mindedly only of my struggle as a Greek, never paid much time to finding out. I assumed the Irish had it made, and I, the Greek, was not supposed to rock the boat.

In 1997, I had an opportunity to travel to Ireland, learning all about the potato famine and how the English kept the Irish held down for many years. If "Irish lads" immigrated to America, their families never saw them again. They were within an era wherein they put in all their effort to withstand "the struggle to survive." I was told their farewell party from Ireland to America was called an "American Funeral Party," because relatives knew they would never see them again.

Get rid of your hang-ups. It does not matter whether you are Jewish, Afro-American, Polish, Puerto Rican, Filipino, Spanish, Italian, German, Asian, or Greek. All had relatives, who at one time or another, have been mistreated, and abused in many ways by one group or another.

There will always be someone to blame for holding someone else back. I cannot make it because my parents divorced, and on-and—on-it goes. Where the blaming will stop no one knows.

The point is, the sport of "blaming" enables a person to become a quitter, to lose focus, therefore, allowing himself or herself to climb up on a shelf, to put it bluntly—to quit.

In order to survive, one must believe in freedom of choice as a chance to reach a goal, and achieve what is really wanted. Opportunity is here in America.

The world is only good to the individual as the individual input makes it. No matter what color, race, or religion, nor matter what other cards may have been dealt to a person since birth, the person's life remains theirs. Go for it!

How about that luck of the Irish? Italian? Afro-American? French? German? Chinese? Vietnamese? And the so-called luck of all the other members of humankind, America is a country of all immigrants each one has a story to tell. Does luck, or nationally, have anything to do with success?

Darrel Royal, head football coach of the University of Texas during the '70s, said, "Luck happens when preparation meets opportunity."

Message #10
No Toilet

BARE ESSENTIALS OF SUBSISTENCE

Let me go back to the 'no-toilet' era in my life. It was a bit comical at times.

I knew nothing about outhouses, never heard anything about septic tanks. I was a city boy definitely used to indoor city plumbing—not outhouses. I didn't realize the five sheets of plywood of my first office were the exact same dimensions as an outhouse; others passing by called my attention to this fact.

I was so focused on getting my business started, I didn't think twice about this need. I knew from my previous sales employment, I needed a catalog and a phone, and at least one sample. That's all I thought about.

Remember, we all have to start somewhere, and when assets are nonexistent or limited, one starts with a dirt floor. Take it or leave it. I stuck it out. This was my business and I was proud of it.

Downside: No water, sewer, or gas lines at that time—I never anticipated this need. All I had was the phone line.

Upside: Lots of trees, bushes, and vegetation. Oh yes, I had toilet paper, a very important necessity at that time.

I made phone calls in that little "out-office."

I could leave my door open in the summertime, feel the warmth of summer, observe the changing colors in the fall, bear the cold of winter, and witness the trees blossom in the spring. I felt as though I was a part of the forest, sharing the facilities with all the four-legged living creatures, contributing to nature in one form or another.

My wife planted a few flowers for me but, unless it rained, they died from lack of water and good soil. It was the best I could do at the time. I laugh about it now, but would dread going through it again. I can only tell myself, "Wow, Spiros! You surely were determined."

I soon began building a cement block plant. Each block cost seventy-five cents and twenty-five cents to lay in place. It was the beginning. Slowly, the roof and walls went up at the rate I could afford to buy the cement blocks.

First Employee:

A young man out of a machine trade school applied for a job and became my first employee. He was hired beginning the next day at 8:00 a.m. At 10:00 a.m. he came to my "office" to find out where the toilet was.

I handed him a roll of toilet paper and said, "Out there," while pointing towards the wooded area. "Pick any tree you want."

"You're kidding, aren't you?"

"Nope. I've been doing this for several months now. If you don't like it, go down to the unemployment office and find another place to work."

Surprised and somewhat laughing at that whole conversation, he stayed. He figured if I could handle it, he could. He and I both found out the real meaning of "cold ass."

Later, people volunteered information about putting in septic tanks. I was a city boy – knew nothing about septic tanks. Since there was no sewer line to the property, I put in a septic tank and installed a toilet in the corner of my cement block plant. I ran a garden hose for water 300 feet to a house at the bottom of the hill.

I had problems with the setup, the hose froze in the winter, and the neighborhood children punched holes in the plastic hose with an ice pick. I guess they had nothing better to do, and thought it was fun making my main water line a sprinkler. To them, it was fun. For me, it meant purchasing regularly another 100-foot length garden hose. Oh well, it was only a temporary situation, right? This situation would change some day.

Message # 11
Positive Thinking

I was poor and feeling sorry for myself. All I had was self-pity, disgust, and a nasty attitude with plenty of negative thinking. While driving one day, I came across a sign near a church. With such truth and simplicity, it affected my way of thinking, it read:

I FELT BAD BECAUSE I HAD NO SHOES UNTIL I MET A MAN
WHO HAD NO FEET.

It led me to the thought that sometimes it is necessary for each of us to be confronted with a situation where there are who have, by fate, definitely been cast into a much more "down-and-out" situation than what we could ever foresee within our own future.

Our problems can be solved one way or another if we develop a positive attitude pertaining to whatever we confront within our short life span on this earth. This means not only in business, but our personal lives as well.

A good attitude accompanied by positive thinking will definitely help you get along better with family, friends, employees, and business associates. Try to remember there are other things in life besides work. Relax, think clearly, and then make your decisions.

There is no end to what you can accomplish with positive thinking.

There are several books on "The Power of Positive Thinking." Get one, and not only read it, DIGEST IT.

Message # 12
Positive Inner Strength

To live is to learn. That is why we are all here. Thus we continue running around this terrestrial planet, trying over and over again, receiving chance after chance, to learn our lessons—to do things the right way.

We must learn to be compassionate, live in harmony, and to truly love. The ultimate lesson we learn is that we must live our lives to the fullest and experiment as we go forward with everything we do. We may go astray at times, making mistakes, having accidents, back sliding now and then, but we need to get back on the chosen path, ridding ourselves of all impurities, and then continuing our journey which will go on teaching us all about life and how to handle it.

We are learning about good and evil, hopefully tossing aside bad habits. We must select only a taste of life's offerings, savoring the splendor and absorbing all possible goodness.

We should consume within our mind and bodies only what is advantageous to our being. What we believe to be the best in life may not appear in proper perspective. Things are not always as they seem. Perhaps we can do better. In fact, there is always room for improvement. There is no limit as to what goodness we can achieve for ourselves and share with others.

Message # 13
Metal Buildings

Metal buildings are less expensive in America than in any other country in the world. As the song goes "...if you make it in New York, you can make it anywhere." If you make it in America, you <u>can</u> make it anywhere!

You have a golden opportunity being an American. Land costs less in the United States (unlike England and crowded Europe); permits are less difficult to obtain (unlike India or Thailand).

Yes, metal buildings are less expensive than in any other country in the world.

Remember...America is always on your side. You can make it here! Where else can you begin a business with absolutely nothing? Pause for a moment and think you could have been born in Afghanistan. Where else can you secure land? Where else can you borrow money from banks, from the government, or because you served in the United States Military Service.

The above remarks have real depth to them. Businessmen and women from Europe and Asia expressed serious emotion while telling me exactly how fortunate I really was to live and own a business in this country. Several of my friends stopped in Europe because of land costs. Europe is crowded.

Metal buildings in the USA, as compared to Europe, are inexpensive because competition brought the price down. Land out in our vast country, out "yonder" so to speak, is relatively reasonable in price. You always have help from local municipalities regarding zoning laws. They generally grant a variance. Building permits are granted easier since property-tax money will be forthcoming. There may be some resistance, but you will overcome. I had it rough for the first ten years because I could only afford a twenty-foot by thirty-foot expansion (Bare Essentials). I had to go through the process of applying for a building permit ten times. One time it took too long. I poured a concrete floor and machined valves outside (see picture).

Whatever it takes, we do. After all, WE/YOU are fortunate…we live in AMERICA!

God Bless America…

Message # 14
You Think You Have It Tough

This picture hangs in my office.

At the time this picture was taken, I could not get a building permit. Therefore, we placed boring mill on concrete pad and machined our valve (note snowflakes - they are real).

Six months later I got my building permit. At last my dream came true!

This is America. This is an American Dream…to build a business, expand, and hire more people.

The above incident is true, not fantasized. After all, non-fiction is truer than fiction!

I did manage occasionally to sing Onward Christian Soldiers to keep up my morale only because this loneliness that I felt within; I certainly needed some sort of boost. Words to this song are next. Please sing it also loud and clear for everyone and all angels to hear. It will help you! When you have a down day, Believe me!

ONWARD CHRISTIAN SOLDIERS

Onward Christian Soldiers, marching as to war.
With the cross of Jesus, going on before.
Christ, the royal Master, leads against the foe;
Forward into battle see His banners go!

Refrain

Onward Christian Soldiers, marching as to war
With the cross of Jesus going on before.
At the sign of triumph Satan's host doth flee'
On then, Christian soldiers, on to victory!
Hell's foundation quiver at the shout of praise;
Brother's life your voices, loud your anthems raise.

I never memorized it all. The first two stanzas picked me up.

Message # 15
Theory of Relativity

A hobo is somewhat of an entrepreneur, a vagrant, a migratory worker, and a person who hops trains. This hazardous transportation, hopefully, would transport him to some new, exciting places, maybe a small town in which to escape from reality a farm, or a city in which one could find employment.

There are various hobo descriptions.

My father, who had just come from the old country, could not find employment in Springfield, Massachusetts; Pittsburgh, Pennsylvania; or Richmond, Virginia. Circumstances warranted that he hop the next freight train, traveling to Iowa, obtaining a job breaking rocks in a stone quarry. You could not label him a true hobo or bum but instead, an "entrepreneur."

He became almost a professional in hopping trains and eventually got himself a job as a brakeman. What is a brakeman? Before **Westinghouse Air Brakes**, a brakeman would hop from one car to another turning manual brakes to put the brake on the wheels of the train going down hill, and unwinding the brakes while going uphill. This is what my dad did all day for quite a number of years.

The name "hobo" came from the migratory worker, a person who hopped trains with a hoe and went from farm to farm to do seasonal work.

This is my theory of relativity. Are you a hobo or an entrepreneur?

Message #16
My First Business Experience

A PENNY

At age fourteen I had a paper route. One of my customers had a twenty-four-cent newspaper bill and paid me a quarter. I did not have a penny change so the man told me to go and get change and come back. I walked eight blocks to get his lousy penny change. This became an isolated incident, but an experience I will never forget.

Another one of my customers turned out the light bulb in the hall before handing me change, which included a button, the size of a dime in substitution of a real dime.

I gave up this paper route because my shoes developed holes faster the I could earn money to repair them.

Start a worthwhile business—pass up the newspaper route.

I do not necessarily mean all you people who are working hard drop delivering or picking up newspapers utilizing your own car or those of you driving and escorting a son or daughter who are delivering papers to earn school money. This is different. I am speaking to those adults who deliver papers for a living but do not WANT to be working with no profit because they are not being reimbursed for gasoline they have to purchase. You use your own judgment as to what you are actually happy doing within your lifetime. Why mop floors? Why deliver papers? Why wait on tables? Is there nothing better for you to do?

Let's put it this way. I never quite made it to the Old Newspaper Boys Club, but I made it in business world. I am a success in my chosen profession.

Message # 17
Business Decisions

LIST YOUR NEEDS, and or what decisions you must make:

I have a good product.
I do not want to get involved with partners.
Spend only what I need to achieve my objective.
Bare Essentials of Subsistence
Catalogues
Stationery
Garden Hose
Telephone
New Product Announcement
Patterns for Foundries
Castings
Automobile Expenses

Message # 18
BARE ESSENTIALS OF SUBSISTENCE

FEED family and self for the first year.
Make this powerful commitment to yourself.
Get only the Bare Essentials of Subsistence.

Bare Essentials of Subsistence
Bare Essentials of Subsistence
Bare Essentials of Subsistence
Bare Essentials of Subsistence
Bare Essentials of Subsistence
Bare Essentials of Subsistence
Bare Essentials of Subsistence
Bare Essentials of Subsistence
Bare Essentials of Subsistence
Bare Essentials of Subsistence
Bare Essentials of Subsistence
Bare Essentials of Subsistence
Bare Essentials of Subsistence
Bare Essentials of Subsistence
Bare Essentials of Subsistence
Bare Essentials of Subsistence

Message # 19
I'm a Survivor

During the first year, approximately eighty percent of all businesses fail. Of these survivors, twenty-five percent more will fail during the next five years.

Why do the first eighty percent fail? They run out of money the first year to keep the business going, with no funds leftover to eat, much less take care of the family.

Many of them will say, "If I could have stuck it out one year, I would have made it."

They did not know about BARE ESSENTIALS OF SUBSISTENCE.

The next big failure is some thirty-five years later when the founder runs out of steam or had not had the patience to teach sons, daughters, or relatives how to run the business. Overcoming this crisis is discussed professionally in PART IV.

Message # 20
My First Million

The first million in sales came after eleven years. If it takes you that long, you are a survivor.

You've lived well on the way and did what you <u>really</u> wanted to do. Some people say, "Spiros, you are a lucky man. You have a valve business that sells worldwide."

Yep! I made it. Climbing the rock for eleven years to success after starting with only a telephone, desk, chair and FIVE SHEETS OF PLYWOOD.

GET ON THE BANDWAGON—START YOUR OWN BUSINESS.

It is fun and a challenge on the Road to Success.

Message # 21
What is Success?

What is success? There probably are several different meanings for those who are lucky enough to have found it. In my opinion, success is overcoming one's environment. This could mean you are born in a low-income bracket, not only income wise or because of where you live, but most importantly—your mindset has become low as well. Hang-ups, "no outlook for the future," rule your mind like a virus worming its way through the hard drive of a computer.

Your environment could be the people around you.

Success is overcoming your environment and getting rid of the hang-ups you developed and are carrying on your shoulders.

Overcoming our environment—relatives and friends tend to pass along many causes for each of our hang-ups. This environment could be mediocre friends within our own circle. Therefore, our perception is mediocre. You believe everyone is in this environment because they and you have not had the opportunity to view life's other possibilities, you see life through the same point-of-view as others who travel with you in the same orbit.

I love my parents—good—honest—sincere people who, as immigrants, came to the United States with nothing more than a grade-school education, accompanied by an even greater will and opportunity to earn a decent living and raise their family to know the true meaning of opportunity and freedom.

Both my father and mother taught me the true meaning of opportunity and freedom.

When an individual approaches a much later age in life, he/she then really begins to reflect back, to see the world in its actual prospective—the way it should have been seen. This is the time you realize nobody lit a candle to guide you in the proper direction.

It takes quite some time to become aware of the mediocre circle you live in or a domineering mother you must overcome. There are many other similar forces. Parents living during a depression pass on fear of insecurity to their children.

Got to shake it off.

I have a friend, a successful executive of a large corporation, who confessed he <u>never</u> went into his own business because of the fear of a depression instilled in him by his father's strife.

The probability of an immigrant child growing up to adulthood with hang-ups has always been at an all-time-high rate because there are definitely no other role models within their individual household.

If you are a member of a minority group in the United States the probability of suffering hang-ups definitely increases.

Secretary of State, Colin L. Powell, apparently shed his hang-ups.

Find a role model.

Suppose you are in an old school, farmer-household where the father preaches, "You don't need no book learning. All you need to know is farming. Farming is your whole life." Any books brought into the house were generally thrown into the fireplace. Sons during that era were definitely brainwashed, believing there was only one occupation in life whatever <u>his</u> father learned from <u>his</u> father and so on.

There was nothing more to be said regarding the subject of a boy's abilities. He was prohibited from having any brainpower.

Thank God things have changed, although there are some fathers, who like the early settlers, refuse to allow their sons to follow any occupation other than the family tradition.

Daughters were no different in that they were taught to cook, sew, make candles, get married at an early age, have babies (boy babies preferred to work on the farm,) do the canning, clean house, help with whatever their man wanted, and Lord knows how much more. Nevertheless, there were no chances here. Male and female roles had been firmly set. You did what you had to do within your circle.

Ignorance may have been bliss back then, but not today. We have come out of environment partially, but it is up to you to go the rest of the way. During this day and age, there are many opportunities out here being offered to young people who are willing to "go for it."

You do not have to listen to anybody when you reach college age (generally eighteen.) work if you have to, get a scholarship if you can. If your father is stubborn and wants you to do one thing and you prefer another, do not please your father. Unhappiness will follow you in a profession in which you will not be happy.

It is you who must be working for what you believe in, what you really want to do, and not chose because someone else wants that for you; do not chose because it may sound good to others, but chose because it is what you really want.

My parents were from Greece. I later realized their friends, extinct volcanoes, and people relating to stories about the "Glory of Greece" back in 200 BC, the Parthenon, my entire magnificent heritage, surrounded me. They came to America to seek gold, and many found glorification only in reminiscing about their homeland's past. That they where descended from "good stock" dating back to the "Golden Age of Greece."

That did not get me good grades—hard work studying and a goal were needed.

You have got to be mentally prepared for challenges of a new business and need a lot of self-confidence. That is why I am relating my problems throughout this book. Samuel Johnson, a great thinker of the past, said, "Self-confidence is the first requisite to great undertakings."

Beware of hang-ups.
THINK SUCCESS!

The previous section can be summarized as follows: 1) there is a need to know what one really wants to do with the skills, education, resources, and business concept he or she has to start the journey. 2)

The need to know that bare essentials of subsistence requires sacrifice. 3) The need to know that staying focused on the goal (what one really wants) means eliminating hang-ups and distractions.

Questions serve the purpose of focusing on the directions necessary for problem solving. Before beginning the next section entitled, THE USE, think about the direction you want to go by answering the most important question, "What do I really want?"

PART II

<u>THE</u> <u>USE</u>

The lessons of THE USE section I learned the hard way, but not necessarily through the method of trial and error. I expect to falter, make mistakes, even fail sometimes, but I do not plan to. If I stay focused on making THE RED VALVE COMPANY competitive in the market place by providing the best marketing campaign of product, materials, workmanship, and service support—all provided within a competitive price—I know I will succeed—

Spiros G. Raftis.

Lesson # 1
Advertise

"DOING BUSINESS WITHOUT ADVERTISING IS LIKE WINKING AT A GIRL IN THE DARK, YOU KNOW WHAT YOU ARE DOING, BUT SHE DOES NOT."

In order to be successful, I had to let industrial plant operators know that I was manufacturing a new-style valve for hard to handle liquids and powders. Even with mousetraps, people must know you're manufacturing the best, most unique mousetrap with many advantages.

I had little money for advertising.

I knew that industrial trade business magazines inform readers in their "new products" section about the latest innovations. My best course of action, therefore, was to spend what little funds I had on photographs, literature for new product releases, and promotional activities rather than purchase machinery, office equipment, or services of a staff at the beginning.

Create a need first.

I repeat this over and over again, one of the main reasons for failure of small business is depletion of cash flow, which means, cash spent on machinery, desks, and computers. One actually runs out of funds, not necessarily because they didn't have enough to begin with, but because what little cash possessed was not spent wisely.

To get results and clientele ADVERTISE. I let people know what type of business I operated, and what I was offering for sale, Advertise in newspapers, radio commercials, and trade magazines. The word of your new product and enterprise must get out to the business world.

I designed a size 3"valve, on my kitchen table, and then made a sample, which I photographed galore. I forwarded these photographs with an announcement to editors of new product releases.

News releases became my main effort.

Inquiries soon began coming in from all over the United States from both users and industrial distributors. I later gave drawings of other valve sizes to pattern makers, bought the castings and "farmed out" the machining of the valves. I didn't need lathes. I needed advertising and orders.

Whatever cash I had left was spent printing a catalogue— expounding the features and advantages of my valve, which I designed, patented, and was unique enough to develop a new market. As more literature went out, quotation requests for prices began to flood my desk. What was even more important was getting calls from manufacturer representatives, and industrial distributors across the country wanting to sell my valves. I needed sales representatives who could sell the need, use and value of my product.

FREE PRODUCT releases pay off. I spent money on catalogues, not on elaborate manufacturing facilities.

My facility, **FIVE SHEETS OF PLYWOOD**, was sufficient.

Lesson # 2
My First Piece of Production Equipment and What I Manufacture

JUNKYARD EQUIPMENT

I went to the junkyard to see if I could get someone's discarded equipment. Fortunately, I found a medium sized lathe without an electric motor (which was extra).

I offered the junkyard owner $75.00.

"Weight of material as scrap is worth more than that," he bellowed.

"Ah, come on. I really need that lathe. Give me a break. I just started a new business, and now you refuse to sell me the lathe, which I need to make a living? I'm broke! That's all I have!"

"If you're that hard up and really need this lathe, then take it."

I even talked him into delivering it a half-mile away in his dump truck. He agreed as long as I took full responsibility in case it cracked when dumped on the ground.

Getting it to run was another problem since it was belt driven. I bought a drill press from **Sears and Roebuck™**, and was now able to do a little machining. This started me on the manufacturing side of the business.

Today I own five CNC machines ($900,000 each). That $75.00 junkyard lathe started it all.

Incidentally, when I relate some of these lessons people ask, "What do you manufacture?"

I manufacture a valve that is basically a rubber hose that pinches close. It is made in sizes 1/8" diameter to 120" diameter. Some valves are so large a person can walk through them. The valve can be closed with a hand wheel, with air on the outside, an air cylinder, or an electric motor in all of the above sizes.

All variations are designed for customer's needs. Customer's need also was instrumental in designing and manufacturing an all-rubber-check valve that became my best seller.

Because a rubber hose that is pinched closed has no pockets (for food decay,) radioactive slurries, storm water—which carries branches, plastic, and metal cans—will not jam up.

Pinch valves uses include, mining slurries, sewage, sludge, flour, and sugar—all hard-to-handle materials—that will plug a conventional valve. I got started in pinch valves after I saw a version of a manual-operated pinch valve. The possibilities of its uses intrigued me for it was being made only in small sizes. Since I had spent the previous five years selling seven different styles of valves to industries, I saw the distinct advantage of a "Pinch Valve, and rather than procrastinate I DID IT.

I saw the potential of closing this rubber hose manually, with air, electrically. I visualized the need for large sizes starting at 12 inches and over. I was confident in making it as a manufacturer because all seven of the different-styled valves I sold before were of little-known companies, and they had made it big.

How many people see similar needs, and sit on them—DO NOTHING.

I REACHED BACK FOR POSITIVE REASONS TO SUCCEED.

I REACHED BACK FOR POSITIVE MOTIVATION.

Lesson # 3
Phase Two in Business

HORNETS NEST:

I had my office, land, and factory. One would say I had it all.

This is all I could afford. It served the purpose. What little money I had was put into printing more catalogs for customers. I also needed to write letters to trade journals for a free ad in—**New Product Releases**—a trade magazine about the exceptional features of the valve I was about to manufacturer.

My market was directed to industrial users nationwide.

No customer would be visiting my general office(s) so "image" was not one of my priorities.

The funniest thing I recall in the five-sheets-of-plywood office was the day a hornet came in while I was on the phone with a client. The only "hornet weapon" I had was a shovel used to dig the foundation. I requested that the customer on the other end of the line hold on for just a moment. I killed the hornet with the shovel—Bang, Bang! Thump, thump!—not realizing the resounding noise this made on a four foot by four-foot plywood cubicle.

"Hello, hello Spiros? What's happening?"

"It's alright now." I was a little out of breath. Swatting hornets certainly is not an easy task. A fellow in my situation could certainly get bit many times over.

"Why are you panting? Did something happen? Sounded as though the building was caving in."

"No, I'm okay. A hornet just buzzed his way into my office. I had to get rid of it."

"Did you get bit?"

"No, sir. Not even close. I killed him with a special tool I have here in the office."

"Good, good. What kind of tool might that be?"

"Kind of like a metal fly swatter."

"Oh. Well, let's get back to business."

He hadn't a clue that I really meant "my plywood cubical" when I referred to my office.

The other reflection I remember vividly was that I often reminisced on my life on the road for over five years as a salesman meeting people, eating lunch at great restaurants, and enjoying Old Fashions and Martinis for lunch...this I referred to as THE GOOD LIFE.

Now, here I sit...all by my lonesome on top of a steep hill, gazing at my acre of land as I wait for the phone to ring in reply to my new product releases in industrial magazines.

I also had the feeling all I needed was a monk's robe. I certainly spent a lot of time in my tiny little area alone, like a monk, hoping and praying for orders.

I was driven, assured that I would make it in the value manufacturing business. It must have showed. A friend of mine stopped by at the time and after listening to me said.

Spiros when you where born the doctor rather than slap you on your ass took an "Armours meat stamp" that said Value Manufacture. Incidentally I never forgot his quirk. I guess it showed.

Lesson # 4
Business Decisions

LIST YOUR NEEDS, update the list:

I have a good product.
I don't want to get involved with partners.
I spend money only when I need to achieve my objective.
BARE ESSENTIALS of SUBSSISTENCE:
Catalogues
Stationery
Phone
New Product Announcement
Patterns for Foundries
Castings
Septic Tank
Automobile Expenses

Lesson # 5
Hiring Employees

I was now in my third year of a new business, and had hired a secretary whom I trained specifically to answer any technical questions and phone inquiries. There were now two men in the shop since sales began to pick up considerably. What a traumatic experience during those first two years. Going on the road for one week, and then rushing back to supervise the manufacturer of the valves.

I wore a cool-dude hat, remained suave, dressed like a professional salesperson, as well being the gallant conversationalist on the road, explaining engineering features with a glib manner. Maintain all the attributes of a professional salesperson. Uppermost, being a congenial friendly guy—helpful—cool.

Next week, back at the shop—direct opposite personality—crack the whip.

Next step was to hire a valve design engineer as the business continued to grow, and customers needed variations—new designs.

A valve designer complete with a Professional Engineer certificate applied for the job. He had six years of design experience with a well-known national valve company. I questioned him about his last job, and he informed me that he was let go.

"Why?"

"Because I love hunting I applied for a hunting license in Wyoming for elk, and big-horn sheep. Licenses are raffled, in Wyoming. You purchase a "hunting license raffle ticket." If they pull your license in the raffle you get to go hunting. Otherwise they refund your money. Well, I won! I went to ask my boss for the time off."

"Then what?"

"He said that if I had vacation time left, I could go. If not, well...that's why I'm applying for this job."

"What happened?" I thought, *This guy's a bit different. He is definitely not the conventional type of employee. He makes up his own mind. I like that.*

"I'm here. Because I went hunting anyway."

I offered him a job, and explained that I couldn't afford a large base pay, but could pay him an attractive incentive. Five percent override on all orders from sewage treatment plants nationwide. He stated that was an unbelievable incentive.

"When can you start?" I asked.

"Well, I really wanted first to go hunting and fishing for at least four more months."

"How can you afford to take this much time off work? Didn't you say you are married and have three children?"

"Yes, however, in my mind, I decided, several years ago, all bosses are bastards. I managed to save one year's salary, just in case, I didn't want to work for some bastard."

Wow! Here's a guy with three kids, and has one year's salary in the bank, he sounds almost unbelievable.

I actually found myself half apologizing for the pressure I was putting on him.

Well, two weeks later he called. "Tell you what. I'll begin work for you right away. I cannot turn down an incentive offer like that."

"Sounds good to me. Look forward to working with you." He seemed happy enough to show up in two weeks, which he did.

He became a big asset to the business by designing and redesigning products, making presentations to consulting engineers, developing a slide cassette presentation, building sales to the sewage market. He made money not only for himself, but for my company as well, and spent time working extra hours at his home. Talented people often work harder than what is required. We worked as a team. I learned valve design during this period.

A small business can use a person with a mind of his own who does not fit within a normal corporate structure; a person who forces someone to take notice of him during the interview, someone who looks at the world in a quite a different way, often, a progressive way, a sincere employee towards his work.

The man was an asset to my newly formed business, and I repaid him with honesty, trust, and money.

Lesson # 6
Ask for Advice

It is a good idea to ask people in the same business for advice.

Before getting started in the valve business, I decided to start a pipe fabricating business in a garage. I got an order to fabricate long lengths of pipe for an oil refinery in Texas. It seemed like a great business, but I needed advice. I drove by a pipe fabricating shop, and stopped to speak with the owner. I explained that I was starting a pipe fabrication business and asked his advice.

"Come to my shop this afternoon at 1:00p.m."

Imagine asking advice from a competitor. I met him at the proper time. He was very honest with me as he began to explain problems, and battles I would have to overcome—**Steam Fitter's Union**—welding codes, and a myriad of other complex encounters.

I kept thinking this is a man who frankly tells another exactly what to expect, a person who could be a competitor. I admired his sincerity.

Try it! Walk in someday and say, "I want to start the same business you have."

Try it; the shock of learning good, truthful advice astonished me, as it will anyone. It seems people do like to talk about their business, their industrial aches and pains, as well as the good side of things.

I followed my own advice recently and contacted another first-time writer for advice. He sure helped me.

Years ago, I read Dale Carnegie's, **How to Win Friends and Influence People**. He mentioned it was human nature for people to help others with advice. I recommend this book as part of your own notes and learning material for success. It definitely is a *must-read*. I have re-read parts often.

I didn't get into pipe fabrication in a big way because of his advice. I knew valves not pipe fabrication. Know the product, service, or both, and then work on what is known. Always get into a business you know about. If not, one may run into a brick wall, and get hurt in more ways than one.

Lesson # 7
Partners—Outline Divorce Papers First

WHY NOT PARTNERS?

A business partner is a marriage without love. Forget about a prenuptial agreement, go further, and prepare a divorce agreement with your partner before you start.

Partnership—Get Divorce Papers First

Fred was the top salesman in the men's clothing department of a large department store, and wanted to open up his own haberdashery. Not having enough capital to invest in his business venture, he discussed finances with his best friend, Herbie, who offered complete financial backing for the entire venture.

Together they found an empty storeroom, purchased $50,000 worth of inventory (in 1953 that was a large sum of money) and opened a business selling men's clothing. What a union! It seemed as though together they possessed all ingredients for a successful partnership.

Not so.

Two weeks after they opened the store, Fred complained about the constant pressure, long hours, losing sleep, worrying about paying the rent, his low take-home pay, loss of vacation time earned while employed at the department store, not to mention the lack of required medical benefits.

Fred, not exactly the epitome of honesty during this transaction with Herbie, finally admitted he never actually quit his job at the department store, but was merely trying this new business venture during his two week's vacation.

"Sorry, Herbie. I just can't handle all this. Too much pressure. I need to get some sleep!"

Herbie could be heard for miles as he screamed. "What the hell are you talking about? I laid out $50,000 for inventory. I helped you get into a business that could be a major success and you're worried about losing sleep? Fred reminded Herbie he is a 50/50 partner, and he had better calm down and quit his screaming.

Poor Herbie. He had to buy Fred out…good old Fred. He had lost nothing but sleep since he had nothing invested monetarily. He got paid to quit.

This may sound like a far-fetched story, but it actually happened, and continues to happen more often than not. Before forming a partnership, make a written agreement, even if it's scribbled on a piece of paper. Outline a divorce.

The need of an agreement was brought to light later in my career, involving the manufacturing business. I hired a manager whom I met in California. I was impressed with his sales and management experience, got carried away, and told him during the interview that if things worked out, meaning sales tripled or quadrupled, I'd eventually give him ten percent of the company.

During the second interview, he told me that he thought a lot about my offer and wanted to ask one more question.

"This ten percent of stock."

"What about it?"

"Will I actually get the stock as soon as I begin employment?"

"Not exactly. The stock deal would require that you stay with the company for five years, and then you would receive two percent of company stock each year."

"Why don't you give me the stock when I begin the job? Don't you think I'm worth it? Don't you have any confidence in me?" He was definitely perplexed.

"I do have confidence in you, but what if you quit six months later with ten percent of the stock in my company."

He still could not understand why I didn't trust him so I related to him the story of Fred and Herbie.

My mistake with this employee from California was that it was all verbal—no sheet of paper.

His impression was that he would eventually receive as a bonus, more stock in the company. All of this was verbal. He only heard the parts of the offer he liked best. After five months, he didn't progress at all; I fired him. He sued me, claiming he moved to Pittsburgh because of my offer and was set back financially.

Let me insert this:

I did not write and confirm the terms of employment. I didn't even scribble anything regarding this position on a piece of paper, photocopying it for my files.

The little venture cost me $55,000 in lawyer fees and damages of $30,000, in 1970. Muttering and calling him every name in the book certainly didn't help as I wrote him a check. This was indeed a bitter pill to swallow. I had to digest my pride on this one, and pencil it in under my lessons-learned-the-hard-way column. Do not ever make the same mistake; the entire business might be at stake.

I never did get another partner—other than my adult children who later became my only partners. This is one bit of advice my father told me—DON"T GET A PARTNER. It is better to have half a loaf of bread. One can eat the half the loaf without asking permission.

It took me twice as long to get there without a partner and I am not sorry.

I made my mistake, but I learned; not to say that there were not other overtures.

I also contacted a venture capital source. WOW! They wanted 50% ownership for a very nominal amount of money.

Another person later who was very qualified, he had some cash, and he was interested in becoming my partner. I felt somewhere along the line he would develop an overrated opinion of his ability and then want concessions. He also probably, in turn, would feel I had an overrated opinion of my talents and we would clash.

I also felt I already had one partner—Uncle Sam—who is a non-working, silent partner. He costs me enough.

Lesson # 8
What Wages to Pay Employees

Wages and what to pay employees...sounds so simple but the truth of the matter is that many battles are lost right on this point.

PHASE 1

When starting a business, pay what you can afford to clerical assistants; hire a high-school graduate with no experience. I was amazed by how many students who took an academic course were good at shorthand and typing. They were eager to work, and needed to gain experience in the business world. It does require much patience on your part, as these were young people who never worked before, and found it a little difficult adapting to work hours and self-discipline.

Regarding accounting services, I found it favorable to hire a retired accountant. He would accept less pay since he was already receiving a pension and/or social security.

Everyone else I hired was of the young and inexperienced class. It was a team of incompetent people who were paid a minimum wage. All the machinists were graduates of local trade schools with no experience. Together we muddled through each day.

This makes life tough for the entrepreneur initially as he/she must constantly train, watch and correct everything that is done. This is reality. You can't afford to pay good wages to competent personnel, so you spend a great deal of time supervising, training and being patient.

PHASE 2

When business gets better, hire college graduates. Hire an engineering graduate, but even then, try to keep the base pay low with a possible incentive bonus.

I got real support with the professional valve design engineer I hired. He had ability and sales aptitude. Inside of one year, he was on a bonus basis, ended up staying with me eight years. Together we made a bundle of money, and he loved the work. We made a great team.

Within a year of hiring the engineer, I hired a fresh, out-of-college accountant and a salesperson. It was at this period within my business that I could afford to hire brainpower.

Plant Manager—about fifteen years later, things were going quite well, as sales were multiplying. I then required the assistance of a good production manager for my rubber operation since my field was a very specialized one. I received a resume from a competitor's plant manager. He seemed reasonably satisfied with the wages and benefits during the first interview. Three months later during the second interview, he requested another seven percent more to accept the position. I replied that I did not want to get into a bidding war with his present employer.

He said he had requested more money from his previous employer after the last interview but was turned down. In fact, he was told to go take the job offered by me. This irritated him for he knew his value. He said, "I made lots of money for him."

Thus, I had my new plant manager who was trained and good at what he did. I got my competitor's plant manager with ten years' experience. Moral of this story is: don't be cheap when the right person arrives. If that employee is making money for you...*PAY HIM WELL!* I am indeed lucky to have personnel that bring in the proverbial "bucks." Do not make the mistake of losing a good person to one of your competitors.

Lesson # 9
Agreements

When in doubt, make an agreement! If liability is high, make an agreement. Whenever large funds are involved, make an agreement.

For example, a job interview agreement, the candidate has impressive credentials, charm, knowledge, and professionalism.

Conventional wisdom may say, "We need someone like you on our team and eventually you may become an owner. That is, if you bring in two million dollars worth of business, we will pay five percent override and maybe give you stock within our company." Perhaps after a two-martini lunch the candidate accepts your offer.

STOP RIGHT THERE!

People hear what they want to hear. The owner said five percent override on sales, NOT five percent of the business. To repeat myself, *people hear what they want to hear, terms they like—it actually is not dishonesty on their part as they do some dreaming, too.*

Put the offer in writing. If not typed, write it all out on a sheet of paper, date it and give the prospective employee a copy. Tell he/she to come in for another interview to review job duties and objectives.

All it takes is a sheet of paper stating salary, perks (car, clubs, etc.), ownership (if any), and terms. Tell the candidate to look the agreement over carefully and bring it back upon his return.

If it is an agreement for contract work, for example, state, "I will pour one thousand yards of concrete for $16,000 plus material. Add to this: (1) Work to start in ten days, (2) completion within thirty days. Request a copy of the liability insurance policy.

A single outline letter agreement, even handwritten, will hold up in court.

Believe me when I tell you—*people hear what they like to hear—* the terms agreed upon must have mutual understanding.

Lesson # 10
Location

People in business say that the most critical aspect of a retail business is LOCATION, LOCATION, and LOCATION. Go directly to the proposed location and attempt an hourly count of passers by. In fact, take two weeks to do this traffic/body count. If the body count is low, search for another location.

I asked a very successful businessman what he considered the most important aspect in starting a retail business. He replied,

LOCATION
LOCATION
LOCATION

The next critical issue is terms of the lease. Make certain the rent can be paid. The landlord makes out, and he's off the hook by pushing you into a five-year lease with a five-year option. This is mega bucks even at $500.00 a month.

When the ideal location is found the need shifts now to finding an attorney who can draw up a favorable lease, or disaster looms. A quick mental note here about a good attorney: *Ask around town in an attempt to find a professional attorney who deals in real estate as a specialty because real estate laws are a specialty and change frequently. Lawyers keep throwing new curves into leases. The only way to survive any of this is to find that extra-special real estate attorney!* You'll be glad you did!

At this point you must again determine what type of business you will enter. For example, the greeting card business.

I asked a friend, "Why did you select greeting cards as a business?"

"I am a CPA, and I feel working as a CPA is not a good future for me, so I began investigating various businesses and their profit making futures. At first, I thought of being a beer distributor but found the profit margin low, maybe $1.00 per case. I would have to sell a lot of cases of beer at $1.00 profit to make $55,000."

"Then what did you do?"

"I did my own market survey, spending over two months talking to people, going to various businesses for advice." This is the key phrase—asking for people's advice in any given area. They will be truthful and glad to share their experiences, both good and bad, with you. I cannot stress enough the importance of advice from successful business people!

I have a friend who owns four hotdog shops, a retail business, all successful. He negotiated and rewrote leases, in some cases six times, to get <u>survival</u> <u>terms</u>. He taught me the word location, location, location, and its importance to retail business.

If the hot-dog or greeting card businesses represent first-time ventures delay opening either store until location and profitability can be determined. If it is a new field, consider going to work for someone within that particular business, after one month, a decision can be made as to whether or not the business is doable and you really like it.

Lesson # 11
Insurance

Are you saying you can't afford life insurance? That is a personal problem? I never carried life insurance (other than a $10,000 policy) for the first ten years I was in business.

I could not afford to pay premiums on a $200,000 life insurance policy. Product and comprehensive liability insurance, however, is a <u>must</u>. Without it, a claim can end up costing well into your future.

Cost of comprehensive and liability insurance is reasonable because it is based on dollar volume of business. In starting a business, your volume is generally low. Trust me when I tell you to get liability coverage.

Call an insurance agent.

Lesson # 12
Women in Business

Currently, women own twenty-eight percent of all small businesses. They get into a business by inheritance or their own entrepreneurial choice.

The challenges to succeed are the same—overcoming the same obstacles.

One of the most interesting things we have seen happen in the late 20th century is the change in the corporate world because women have begun to take a greater part in it. Service-oriented businesses, which are becoming increasingly important in the innovative information society, are offering unique opportunities for women.

Women are often labor sensitive, requiring little capital, but many hours of work to succeed. Second, they can start on a small scale and build over a time period while developing various skills. Third, they do require the commitment of an entrepreneur. These businesses can be started relatively easy and have excellent growth possibilities.

WHAT ABOUT WOMEN INHERITING A BUSINESS?

Our bank invited my wife and I to a seminar that dealt primarily with women inheriting the husband's business. Many issues were discussed. The two significant revelations were as follows:

Owners of businesses routinely go home and brag to the wife that their business is so great, it's worth two and a half to three million dollars if he sold it. He is making so much money he's definitely going to keep it!

This is a value that, in many cases, is unrealistic, made up 80% for ego satisfaction and 20% profitability.

Upon the owner's death, the widow has difficulty accepting an actual value price to sell the business.

The bank is requested to find a suitable buyer at an inflated price. The bank also, has difficulty in convincing the widow of another major factor; it is much easier to sell a dry cleaning business than a specialized valve business catering to a 'niche' market. How many people know valves?

Women, in many instances, are forced into stepping in and running a business, confronted with all the challenges and issues discussed in this book.

WOMEN EXECUTIVES WORKING FOR A SMALL BUSINESS

I cannot go without mentioning the value of my secretary in my business. In the beginning years of my company's growth, she worked typing, answering phones, the usual secretarial duties. Several years after being hired, it was obvious she was planning on a management career with my firm. She eventually earned the position of Vice President.

I trained her to answer technical questions about my products. Eventually, on another new product, I made her head of the division with an incentive. The new product sales grew, the company benefited, and her compensation grew as well. For twenty-two years this "executive woman" helped my company grow.

She wanted to put her three children through college. My incentive offer paid off. This was her driving force.

Women employees are a vital, important part of any business. They help it grow.

An executive who has not learned this does a grave injustice to his business' and/or the firm's growth.

Lesson # 13
Learn to Listen

My New Jersey sales representative called me to advise me that my newly patented check-valve was terrific but it only goes to size 12", and he had a customer who required a 56" diameter check-valve for storm sewers. I told him to forget it as I'm having trouble with making a good 12" valve that works.

Two weeks later, he called me once again asking about a 56" valve. I had to reply, No! No! No! Two weeks after that he insisted I visit the EPA in New Jersey in order to hear what the customer had to say regarding the need of a very large-sized, check-valve.

When speaking with this particular customer, I explained that I only made the new valve product up to a 12" size and presently have some problems producing even a 12" size. This customer insisted and wanted to know how much it would cost to design and manufacture the 56" size.

I told him $19,000, but I could not guarantee the production of a good valve that would actually work well, and I would have to build at least two prototypes.

"You got a deal!" He was quite emphatic in his statement, having a purchase order drawn up and telling me to, "Go to work and I know you will make one of the two that'll work for me!"

This product became and is my Number One product, which now contributes forty percent to my total sales.

Learn to listen—sell customers what they need—not what you make easily—or like to make.

You can have the best-engineered product, but if there is no use for it you will not sell it.

Listen to the market.

Listen to the <u>needs</u> of customers.

Expand when you have to, pull back when you must—just keep going.

Learning to listen is very important with employees as well. They are doing a job day in and day out. Their minds and bodies work on your product and business, they are in a position to make or suggest changes you probably will never think of.

Just walk through your office and plant. Speak to the employees often. They are 'best friends,' so to speak, and are working for you as well as WITH you.

Listen to this. A Union Shop Steward, who I disliked, spoke to me one day with a bit of puzzlement. "I can't figure you out! We have a twenty-year-old relic of a forklift, which we spend two days every week fixing, and it takes away two men from production in order to fix it! You are definitely wasting money, don't you think?"

I listened, went back to my office, multiplied two full-day-wage rates times four weeks. I found out that monthly payments on a new forklift would be less than what it cost me to repair that old forklift. Imagine a Union Shop Steward, who disliked me, and I usually fought with, trying to help me.

Incidentally, this incident was also a part of the day-to-day orientation for the next generation, which we will discuss later.

Lesson # 14
Payroll Services

There are numerous firms that offer payroll services including issuing paychecks, taking deductions, and a year-end tax filing. This includes year-end statements for federal income tax, social security, Medicare, local head tax, local city tax, and any other taxing authority, whether local or out of state.

All that is required from the employer is to call in weekly hours and rates for both salaried and hourly employees.

Hire a payroll-service firm. Avoid hours that are spent balancing each of the deductions to the last penny. A typical employer may be filing forms for several surrounding city boroughs, even state taxing bodies.

Payroll taxes are sent direct. All this can be done for a very low fee. Many hours required for this particular phase can be utilized on more profitable business problems. It makes sense to hire a payroll service since it is <u>relatively inexpensive</u>. I do highly recommend it to all entering into a new business. Headaches trying to balance to the last penny on government forms will definitely be spared.

<u>The service is relatively inexpensive.</u>

Lesson # 15
Clarity of Thought

At times, you get to a point when you feel exactly like a juggler, keeping six or seven balls in the air at once. Hey, here come three more. Are there times when you find yourself within a state of absolute confusion? The answer is definitely yes; I was confused at times.

Now, with this new "informational age" it gets much worse.

My solution was to wake up at 5:00 a.m. before the wife and kids, TV, dog, and within my own solitude time ask for CLARITY OF THOUGHT. Let's determine the inner circumference of your problem, considering all the facts as to what may be the *real* issues here. Clarity of thought means just that. Ask yourself exactly <u>what is the most important, pressing thing I can and need to do that day.</u>

It's like making a grocery list, write down various daily errands as well as important matters that really should be completed. My wife practices this method, and is quite coordinated in taking care of groceries, various other supplies, writing checks, gift purchases, cards or flowers, errands, and not to mention keeping the appointment schedule. What isn't quite a necessity or doesn't get done in one day carries over to her list the next day.

You do the same. Pick out the most important items you have to do first for business, and if they take more time than you planned in your schedule, simply place it on the list for the following day. Add and take away. This does help with self-organization. It may take several weeks to get in the groove, but the brain stores information. It is the most refined computer of all, easy to get to, and is great at storing facts. Get "on line" within yourself by asking for "clarity of thought."

Ask what is most important—what should be done first?

Ask for clarity of thought in this over-taxed-information-age.

Lesson # 16
Role Models (They Come in All Ages)

When you are looking to make it big at a rapid pace in the business world, look for a role model to admire, hopefully in your contemplated venture. They are all around you and appear in all sizes, shapes, and age groups.

For years, Nick Mitchell had a fancy fruit stand at the old Pennsylvania Railroad Station in downtown Pittsburgh, just scratching out a living because of the high rent and low traffic. He struggled for most of his life, finally making a go of his business at age 75 during World War II when many of the armed forces personnel were traveling by rail to the various camps. They wanted fresh fruit, personally or as a gift, he, finally, became successful. Imagine busting butt for seventy-five years in various ventures before making something out of your business. He was still trying at age 75 to make it.

And you think you have it tough.

He amazed me. He financed his sons through college. They inherited his money, bought real estate, and are the Yuppies of our era.

I mopped floors, helped wash walls, polished silver and brass, not to mention the errands and other things I had to do. I can now boast of having over thirty patents. My best invention will be the next one. I own a company doing several million dollars' worth of sales.

Go find a role model, or remember seventy-five-year-old Nick Mitchell.

Lesson # 17
Lawyers—Liability or an Asset?

Obtaining good legal advice brings to mind Demosthenes, who with candle in the daylight, was "searching for an honest man." I do not mean that literally. It is difficult to find a good, intelligent, knowledgeable, sincere, and honest person who provides excellent legal service.

The first rule, choose a knowledgeable legal consultant for the special issues, such as, labor lawyers, real estate lawyers, estate planners, corporate lawyers—specialists in their field. Do not pick a lawyer because his firm has a good reputation.

If a mistake is made do not hesitate to change lawyers. Choose someone who will work best for the company, and remember you can stop the clock any time you want.

We are all heartless, in firing manual labor ($5.50 an hour people) with a simple statement, "I won't be requiring your services anymore. Sorry!"

Why should this be different with lawyers? I have personally hired/fired legal advisors mostly because my problem at the time was not their particular specialty or their handling my problem at $150.00 an hour was not satisfactory.

I needed a labor, real estate, patent, and estate-planning attorney to mention a few specialties. Basic rule, choose a legal specialist in the required field. Again, it is important to seek advice, locate the proper "specialist" attorney for your particular needs.

Lesson # 18
Wills and More About Getting a Lawyer

WILLS

Lawyers are important, required, and must be selected properly. My first attempt at making out a Will with my attorney was in 1961. I appointed my brother-in-law, the lawyer who drew up the Will, and the Bank Trust Department as executors—all three. I felt confident that I did the right thing. There were three entities handling my estate. I had three small children and no insurance.

By 1976, the sales for my company had quadrupled. My estate had grown from ground zero to high apple-pie-in-the-sky, forcing me to think about re-writing my Will.

I contacted another lawyer to prepare a more sophisticated Will, with real inheritance tax savings. The lawyer questioned, "Why do you have the bank as executor? The bank's track records aren't very good, especially with small estates. Once they have the trust, it's tough to get the bank out of it."

The Bank Trust Department can lose money or break even, and I would need a lawyer to withdraw my own funds. I eliminated the Bank Trust Department as one of the executors of my estate on this first re-write.

Four years later, the estate got even larger, and I hired another more intelligent lawyer who drew up a more sophisticated Will with bigger tax savings. He suggested that I eliminate my brother-in-law. I agreed.

It was now 1988 and on my third go around, I now was paying $175 per hour to another new attorney.

On his re-write he asked me, "Why do you need an attorney as executor?"

"Well, I answered," I thought everyone needed an attorney for their Will."

"Why? Do you know that if your children begin to fight among themselves, I, as executor, cannot represent them individually or collectively?"

Another small bit of information—all an executor lawyer can say is, "That is not nice, kids," and the lawyer executor collects five percent of your estate for the next fifteen years or until the Will expires for executors of my estate.

Demosthenes! I found an honest man and feel extremely fortunate.

I cannot stress enough how important it is to find a good attorney who is "honest," and change attorneys as needed. Share in the wonderful in-the-nick-of-time-learning experience. Look at the amount of money I saved (5% of my estate annually).

I am not slamming lawyers. Be like Demosthenes, light your lantern and search in all the right places.

Lesson # 19
Hiring an Executive—Confronting S.M.O.A.

Whether it is a marketing manager, chief financial officer, production plant superintendents, or material-handling expert, I discovered that all of these executives possess what I refer to as "large-corporate mentality," the acronym S.M.O.A defines the attitude best. Save My Own Ass principle demands no decisions, because in the event of error the executive goes, not the owner. Instead, the S.M.O.A behavior dictates to the executive to call a meeting, hence—a group decision—whereby no one person can be blamed, least of all the executive.

Financial Officer: I hired one, which resulted with me ending up in dire straits. He decided to lead me into more problems—bankruptcy—enabling him to purchase the company. I saw through his plan before it was too late; I discovered his plan in the morning—let him go after lunch. This really happened leading me into more problems.

Sales Manager: Upon employing this individual, he called later to my attention the fact that he was a marketing man and not used to hiring, training, or firing salesmen, manufacturer representatives, or anyone. For the last twenty years at his former place of employment, he was a marketing man, had to write a business plan and submit it to Chicago, waiting several weeks for a reply. Among other things, he couldn't handle getting an answer from me in two minutes, so he quit. He was not a short-sleeve producer, a sales manager.

Plant Manager, of metal fabricating facilities: I hired this man, from a very large corporation, to get more valves out the door. He advised that he was used to maintaining a staff of people to handle purchase of raw material, flow, order entry system, and performing all the other required functions. All he had to do was answer a few questions whenever things went wrong. If production figures were off, he would tell corporate management that it wasn't his fault the Sales Department is taking orders at a low markup. Corporate management would accept this. Hence, S.M.O.A.

Many large-corporate executives are out of touch with how their business operates. That is why accountants run major corporations for their view of a business is always in black and white. The <u>real</u> business operates in every shade of gray.

Fat-cat executives have extremely bad habits. When they need a new job, in the interview, they do not tell you they can work in the trenches as short-sleeve managers.

<u>Large companies pay fat salaries to executives and employees.</u>

<u>Large corporations are run for the benefit of the employees.</u>

<u>Small companies are run for the benefit of owners and hardworking employees.</u>

Some executives are persons of good intent who just developed a lot of bad habits. They are knowledgeable, but <u>not short-sleeve executives</u>. Their desks seemingly are always cleaned, never anything piled up.

This reminds me of a statement made by the President of a conglomerate, "An executive who has a clean desk is one that is not aware of what is going on and is immune to any of the problems within the company."

NOTHING PENDING.

Lesson # 20
Unions

I went the full route and got hit with union organizing twice. I live in a union mentality town (Pittsburgh). Since unions are strong in this area, one must deal with them openly and honestly, abiding by their rules, cooperating with them in every way.

The first attempt to unionize was with three employees. Yes, three employees! A vote was taken announcing the formation of a union. I contacted a labor lawyer who advised me that I had to draw up a contract with the union, and the cost would be between $15,000 and $20,000 for a standard agreement.

I said, "Ridiculous, for three employees?"

I announced to the workers that I could not afford this nor would I pay this amount of money for a contract to guarantee three people's employment. A picket was threatened. Fortunately, that winter was a cold one, after two weeks of picketing, they all quit.

I would have rather given the employees more money rather than giving money to lawyers.

<u>Second Round</u>: Ten years and eleven employees later.

I was paying the going machine shop wages, had a good employee life insurance policy, hospitalization coverage fully paid by the company, and a profit sharing plan.

I made it a point to treat each employee quite well since I was busy, out-of-town calling on customers and purchasing castings. I needed their earnest cooperation. In doing so, I must have given everyone the shop employees the impression of being a pushover.

A union sprung up.

"Why do you need the union I asked? You are getting a good salary and have good benefits."

"Job security," was the answer given. Such gross Pittsburgh union mentality, all this union stuff for eleven workers, all being in there twenties four years out of trade school; they organized.

I contacted a labor attorney. He quoted $20,000 for the contract, and since I was boiling mad, he said, "Don't threaten workers with firing" Seems it was the Sherman Anti-Trust Act, or something like that. The status of the union went up for a vote.

At that time, my father was working in the shop. I asked my lawyer, "Is he eligible to vote? Does his vote count?"

He replied yes. I wanted to make sure since my father's ballot would be the deciding vote.

On the day ballots were cast, the union representative showed up and challenged my dad's vote. It was invalidated some two weeks later. The union had won its battle.

I was mad enough to visit that attorney who said he hadn't a clue as to what happened at this election.

He replied, "The case took a bad turn for the worse," he said.

I expressed my negative remark that he take his law diploma down from the wall and wipe his you know what with it. That may not have helped my situation in any monetary form, but I did feel better after venting my boiling - point feeling.

The following is a brief list of what I learned and experienced. I was surprised to hear the fact that lawsuits are filed against the union itself. The members of my shop actually did threaten the union business agent with a lawsuit.

One worker became so arrogant that he ran the lathe all day with no cuts, bragging about it to boot.

On another occasion, I had gotten word that one of the employees left his station, went to his car trunk and made a marijuana sale. I questioned him in the office and he denied the charge. He was so nasty that as I walked back to the shop, he screamed "F—you, boss man," and gave me the proverbial finger, which seemed to give him great satisfaction.

I was boiling mad, and I sent him home for one week, no pay.

He filed a grievance with the Union Business Agent who stated that my punishment was too severe. I stated it was my belief that I should have fired him permanently, but I just sent him home for a week. The agent told me, "You can't fire on the first offense or even suspend him for a week."

"When the hell can I fire this arrogant employee, on the second or third offense? By that time, I would lose control of the whole shop by handling things in that manner."

The settlement of the grievance was two and a half days off without pay, instead of, one week.

Three years later, the second round of a union contract.

I phoned another union lawyer and invited him to sit in on the first bargaining sessions.

At that time, I had also started a rubber manufacturing facility in North Carolina. Upon telling my attorney about the NC plant, he wanted to know about its capacity. I told him after two years, it was great and has resulted in over capacity of production.

"Well," he said, "let me handle all the negotiations. And by the way, please do not state costs are lower in North Carolina because the union has the right to check your books. If you have over capacity, you have the right to shut down a facility, but cannot shut it down because of un-profitability. You have to prove un-profitability."

He announced to the Union Representative and Shop Steward that we were closing Pittsburgh's operation, as we did not need that much production.

The Business Agent stood up and said, "Mr. Raftis, you are a gentleman. You could have had my people on the picket line for several months and made the announcement after much suffering out there but told us up front." He looked at the Shop Steward and said, "I guess that's it, boys."

The Union Agent had also been motivated, somewhat, to throw the towel in because of the thirty grievances annually, which eleven people filed along with the lawsuit threat at Detroit. What an ordeal.

As explained previously, search for a sincere attorney specializing in any given field. In this particular case, I needed one for union problems.

Light your lantern then begin to seek and find that honest labor lawyer to handle your union contract.

Can you imagine workers suing the Union? Can you imagine a labor lawyer rendering half-ass advice enabling him to obtain a substantial legal fee, $20,000 for a union contract?

Guardian angel wherefore art thou? Protect me!

Incidentally, the Ohio lawyer informed me of another company that took pictures/slides of plants closed after unionization and displayed these photos to employees. Some closings were after six

76

months, one year, two years, etc. The slides and pictures were presented as a documentary.

Through all this, I am not anti-union. There must have been and will be a need for unions. Generalities are useless. What you do have to watch out for is "Egomaniac Shop Stewards" and "Insecure (stupid) Lawyers." Most often, they are the ones who close good plants, and not the workers or the business agents.

Lesson # 21
Patents

I took a course in college on patents. The instructor repeated and pounded the following:

1. Over sixty percent of the patents inventors are awarded do not pay for the cost of obtaining the patent itself.
2. A patent mainly assures your continuance in making the product yourself that you are producing in lieu of being sued for infringement. Another person cannot stop you from producing it. This is more valuable than stopping someone from copying your invention.

You can regain the cost of getting a patent by deciding that you will manufacture the product. If the plan is to solicit someone to manufacture your product <u>forget</u> <u>it</u>. You are trying to convince someone that he or she could become wealthy just by manufacturing the idea, and that person would invest money and/or manufacturing facilities to make you rich. It would be assuming that the person approached knows how to promote the product, which in all probability, is a niche (suitable) market. It would be assuming that this second party will accept returns, buy advertising, invest in equipment, molds, forms, inventory to make it go for me.

Think this out before you apply for a patent. Who is going to invest his or her capital to make you rich? Remember also, if someone infringes on your patent, the patent office will not protect you. They won't even write a simple letter stating that person is infringing and must cease.

You will have to sue to appear in court with not only good evidence, but an excellent patent attorney as well. The jury will then make a decision if and when the infringement must stop.

The patent office, incidentally, now has sympathy for all those geniuses that lose money getting a patent. Normally it will cost $4,000 to apply for and prepare a patent and $2,000 to $3,000 for first action (reply) of patent office. There is another cost of $1,000 to

$2,000 to receive a final award. The total is approximately $7,000, and unrecoverable if a patent is denied.

US Patent Office, therefore, created a new program entitled "Applying for a Provisional Patent." The initial cost is $1,000 and is good for one year. One can explore the market during that time, and then determine if another $7,000 or more should be spent to obtain a final patent.

If the inventor really loves his' or her's invention, then start a business, apply for a provisional patent, and go for it.

Do not waste time thinking someone else will invest money and time to make you rich.

The best products, the best patents do not assure a successful business.

Lesson # 22
Bankers

I was completely frustrated with bankers when I first started the business for I really needed them.

Basic banking policy: Banks do not lend money to businesses that desperately need it to function properly. Banks only lend money to businesses that <u>do</u> <u>not</u> need it, and have the ability to repay without much effort.

I had to learn all this the hard way. In fact, it has helped me now in dealing with bankers. Be prepared to guarantee the loan personally.

It is at this point that I must agree with the bank. Why should the bank lend someone money who does not want to personally guarantee his own venture? Banks are in business to make a profit, and not to guarantee your venture success.

What if you ask to borrow less money, something you can pay back? The bank might say the loan is so small it isn't worth the paperwork. It's a "Catch 22" situation. Complete frustration.

How long before you personally do not have to sign up for a loan? NEVER!

I have news for you. After being in business for forty-eight years, my wife and I still have to personally sign for a loan regardless of all my company's assets.

Banks do not want your business or its assets.

Banks want their cash back along with a profit made.

Banks are not in the liquidation business.

Ask someone who has been in business whether or not he or she still wake up his wife at 7:00a.m. in the morning and say, "Darling, sign here please." She, at this early in the morning, would almost certainly reply, "I can't see so you'll have to point to the signature line."

In business there are on-the-job conflicts and problems all day long. Finally, arriving home there is always a fresh crisis, or problems with the children. This is reality. Forget that loan application sitting in your briefcase requiring your wife's signature because of all the previous events in the business day causing loss of focus. The wife - signing takes place at 7:00 a.m.

Is it on purpose or subconscious frustration that might make you forget the loan application requiring your wife's personal guarantee?

Expect also a dig—"Am I am signing a divorce agreement?"

The answer lies within.

Lesson # 23
The Restaurant Business

Why reinvent the wheel? Ask for advice.

The restaurant business is a great enterprise. At least I thought so.

I have thirty beautiful acres on the parkway between Pittsburgh and the Airport. I envisioned a rustic looking steak house with ample parking and high visibility from the Parkway. Everyone would want to dine at my five-star restaurant. My valve business was doing well.

I contacted three friends in the restaurant business for which I held very high regard. I felt I had enough savvy to run another business. Having many friends in the food business, including my brother-in-law who sold produce, I invited them to my home for a cocktail party, seeking advice from them regarding my thoughts for a new business—a restaurant.

They told me the first thing I need to do is hire myself on as a dishwasher in a restaurant for one week and see how I like it.

'What are you talking about? I'm going into the restaurant business big time."

"That's what you think. If you get in the restaurant business, and one day while your place is really jumping the dishwasher gets mad and walks out, you'd better be prepared to go back and wash dishes. Because if the chef doesn't have a nice clean dish on which to place his creative endeavor, you're customer leaves! One, two three! A good chef is temperamental." All the waitresses are busy.

"Cut it out! Sounds as though you are trying to discourage me."

"What other obstacles are you going to tell me about?"

"You also better learn to cook. Chefs are all Prima Donnas. You have to cater to their whims, and there is no guarantee they will not leave for a larger restaurant and a more substantial wage, which you couldn't possibly meet.

Let's say you have a dining room full of guests. If you know how to make soup, baked potatoes, steaks, and a few other things, and the chef walks, you can always tell the waitress to inform the customers you ran out of specials, and the only thing left on the menu is broiled steak or fish and baked potatoes."

"I can handle the situation because I barbecue my steaks when we have a cook-out."

"Alright. Go for it! By the way, are you prepared to be 180 degrees out of phase with society?"

"What are you talking about?"

"When you enter the restaurant business many things change, especially at night. Holidays, special occasions, birthdays, time spent with your family have to be ignored because you have to be at the restaurant. No more social or family life in the evening and that's it! Your wife and family will probably carry on with their social activities, but you won't be a part of it. While your family may be out having a good time, you will always be working. They are set to go out.

You are 180 degrees out of phase with society.

Also keep in mind this situation applies weekends and holidays, as well as vacation time. It disrupts not only your personal life, but the personal life of your wife and children as well. So, just be prepared to put yourself on a completely different schedule, never seeing your wife or family at night or when the kids come home from school."

"You've got that all wrong. I am going to run a high-class restaurant recommended by gourmet magazines. I'll have top-notch personnel."

"Let me ask you...name the top four restaurants in the city."

I rattled four right off the bat. They asked me who owned each restaurant? I was very proud that I knew who all the owners were.

"Do you realize you knew all of the owners?"

"Yes, so what?"

"This is a very significant part of the restaurant business. If you want to run a successful gourmet restaurant, you'd better be in that restaurant to shake hands and meet all of your clientele. You like it when you walk into a restaurant and someone says, "Good Evening, Mr. Raftis.' Your guests hear that, and they are impressed; you're quite the man-about-town. This is all part of the big-time restaurant game. The customer always returns when he holds a personal relationship with the owner who has made it a point to remember their names. Big-time restaurant business is built on knowing your clients' or customers' names."

"I can understand that." I did know that being familiar with clientele, supervisors, and plant managers' names are important.

"Another thing, Spiros." (Well, I did ask for their advice.)

"It takes many hours to run a restaurant. If you are not going to be there, the big spenders who bring guests will not return...which brings up another point. If a customer has any particular complaint, they usually want to speak with the owner. This, in turn, gives you the opportunity to pacify him, apologizing for whatever reason. You will either have to offer that customer dessert or buy the drinks or offer him another meal at a future date. Nevertheless, you are there and can do something to keep that customer coming back to your place."

"You guys are really raking me over the coals!"

"No, we're just talking you out of it. We think it's a great business and there's a profit if you handle everything properly. We are merely trying to advise you not to get into the restaurant business part time or without a thorough investigation."

"Anything else you have to tell me?"

"One more thing. If you decide to go to a movie and it's lousy, while walking out you say to your friend, 'What a lousy movie the acting stunk, poor plot, and little or no emotion. However, you will return to the movie theatre again."

"Yeah. I've done that."

"Well, the restaurant business isn't like that. When you leave a restaurant after a bad meal, you'll swear off that place for the rest of your life and, undoubtedly, tell everyone you know about your experience and that you can cook better than that. The restaurant business is really a personal business. When people go to fine restaurants and spend money, they expect superior service, food, and drink. A combination that's hard to find these days."

I got the message. It's a universal language wherein everyone gets the message that if you decide to go into any business, including restaurant, you can't do it part time. Being an owner means all of your time, full time.

Before entering into any business, get all the facts, search for glitches, things that would hinder profit. *EVERY* business requires a lot of personal attention to not only customers, but also how personnel are doing their jobs. Are the orders coming forth within a reasonable time period? Is everyone completely satisfied? Is there any way the owner can improve anything?

Managers, assistant managers, and part-time endeavors can be effective only after a business is established for many years, employees trained for many years, and has a distinguished, well-respected reputation. Remember, full time!

Analyze everything and anything! It is important to note that when you have a family, please take your wife/husband and children into consideration. Ask them what they think. This is important. You might miss your children growing up. This is just a 'beware' sign for your own good.

That's why I suggest being careful in selecting the type of business you want to enter. AND ASK FOR ADVICE.

Restaurants require tough hours away from family.

Lesson # 24
Yellow Belly

When I was working as a sales representative on my first job, I was riding with another salesman from Wheeling, West Virginia, to Pittsburgh, Pennsylvania. During the trip, he told me about how his incompetent, alcoholic, inept boss carried on. He would get drunk and embarrass him professionally. He raved, "My boss is plain stupid!"

Forty minutes later after listening to his whining, I had a chance finally to say something. "You have to be even more stupid than your boss! After all he doesn't work for <u>you</u>, it is the other way around, you work for him. What's your problem? Don't you have enough guts to just up and quit? Go into your own damn manufacturer-rep business. Ever think of that?" You certainly know the business and are smart enough."

I explained to him what an excellent salesman he was. Since he held an Engineering Degree, he could detail in depth to customer's advantages of any technical product. He already had a proven sales record.

As a grand finale in my pitch to give him some gumption, I said, "If they took a knife and cut your belly, yellow puss would come out." Distasteful as these words sound, I felt it necessary to get my point across to a man that needed a push—no, a shove—in the right direction. Sometimes that is all a person requires. His reaction was one of extreme anger, as he verbally exploded, telling me off in no uncertain words.

Fortunately, I saved my advice to when I was outside my home. I slammed the car door when I got out.

He took my advice and, within one year, was in business for himself.

In my opinion, do not wait for someone to call you gutless or a yellow belly. In fact, most people would not even attempt to tell you something like that. This little episode tells you a bit about myself. When it comes to helping others, I definitely got guts—I tell them off! I hate to hear complaints. Blaming others for their misfortunes.

My advice again is to GO FOR IT!

Lesson # 25
The Silent Partner

Advice for a tough meeting or situation coming up, say a prayer and ask God to come in with you as a silent partner. During the meeting when the going gets tough remember the silent partner and say in thought, *They don't know they cannot win because I have my silent partner helping me.* It works believe me. I have used it several times within my lifetime in extremely difficult situations.

As Jesus said, bring your burdens unto me to resolve.

I have talked to several executives and shared this experience with them. Several related to me that they also went into tough rigorous meetings with the same "silent partner," and came out victorious.

God does help and so do prayers.

Try it.

Lesson # 26
A Business Disaster—A Fire

I had a disastrous fire in 1956 that leveled my plant. I was in Philadelphia at the time. One of our employees, therefore, detailed the event. He started by telling me the fire truck stalled outside the fire station for twenty minutes because of engine problems. When it finally arrived at the burning plant, it took another fifteen minutes to connect the hose to the hydrant because it was frozen shut. Finally, thirty-five minutes later, water was reaching the burning building—a bit too late.

By this time, the 440-volt power line got red hot and fell down, cutting the fire hose in half. It took another ten to fifteen minutes to hook up another hose. As fate would have it, my employee informed me the wind then suddenly picked up, fanning the fire at an uncontrollable rate, forceful flames, which spread at a rapid pace. Nothing remained untouched by the fury of that fire. It brought down everything with crashing, blackened disintegration.

The next day, my insurance agent come and assessed the situation. He invited me to lunch. Prior to going to a restaurant for lunch, I asked him to stop, as I wanted to spend a moment at the church to light a candle. My prayer to St. Mary was, "In case you have anything else in mind, I've had enough."

MI XIPOTERA

I just couldn't take anymore. I had worked hard, and within minutes, everything is gone, poofed away by Mother Nature's wrath. How do I handle this without falling apart?

I admit to drinking my lunch that day—three or four vodkas. They failed to relax me. This event was pure hell. There seemed to be no relief or answers.

Many business associates came around that week giving me encouraging words, hopefully, to help me through this situation. They truly were real friends, advising me not to worry about a thing, and

89

perhaps it was for the best because I could now construct a new building and lay out plans for the manufacturing plant the way I really want it rather than the hodge-podge plant I had. I could also buy machinery, get rid of bad inventory. The insurance would pay for everything.

I, however, could only feel my total loss.

Bullshit!

I am wiped out.

A total fire with your business being burned to the ground is *traumatic*. Money isn't the question. Defeat is in there with the loss.

Others said, "Why don't you sell out now rather than rebuild? Your customer following is worth money."

How do you sell a burnt-down business?

More advice was forthcoming from well-meaning friends, bankers, and insurance people.

I went to see my mother, who had a third-grade education in Greece, but being truly wise and knowing her son's every feeling, she sensed that I was nursing self-pity, fear, and defeat.

"Son, I want to tell you an old adage in Greece. Aboard merchant ships, the captain is generally drunk most of the time. The mates actually run the ship. However, when there is a big "Furtona" (violent storm), and the possibility the vessel may sink, they call that drunken sea-faring captain who takes the helm and reveals his "axia" (value) as a captain. Translated, this means he will now, at this possibly disastrous moment, show his worthiness."

I was wiped out to the tune of three-quarters of a million dollars— some of which I owed. I felt depressed as well as defeated. My mother, I thought, was telling me simple fairytales.

On my way home, however, I began to think about her story. What was she really trying to tell me? Simply this—if you really are a capable captain, you will overcome this disaster, and if you aren't a capable captain commanding your business, it will sink.

That's all there is to it.

Her story slowly started putting my loss behind me.

Her advice started giving me self-determination more than all the opinions previously received from bankers, insurance people, and lawyers.

Hell yes, I said. I'm a capable captain and can stay afloat. I will not go down with my ship. I have ability, determination.

Thanks to my mother, I once again had the will to go onward and upward, to rebuild.

Command your own vessel like a true captain during a storm, and say, "AXIOS, I am capable."

Lesson # 27
Why Are You Living?

When the pressure seemed to become heavier than I could bear, I began visiting psychics, fortunetellers, spooks, and took up reading metaphysical books, one of those books being written by Edgar Cayce. His dissertation about reincarnation still stays fresh within my mind. He claims a person's mission on earth is catharsis of the soul, and believes that if one's soul is not clean when death approaches, the person will then be reincarnated, receiving another chance.

I made up my mind. If he is right, I'd best be good because who in the hell wants to go through all this a second time.

I am not a believer in re-incarnation. What I do know is that I do not want to go through all of this again.

Man is a total person of all his experiences and knowledge. If you grow up in a ghetto or a non-intellectual environment, your outlook is totally controlled by these particular surroundings. It is difficult to perceive oneself. Therefore, either move as a turtle, very slow, or react as an entrapped deer, and quickly jump out of it.

My father used to say, "Then Xeris Yati Sis." (You don't know why you are alive). I kept ignoring him, figuring it was just an old time Greek saying. One morning I asked my father for the answer to, "Why am I living?"

"To grow up, my son, and become an honest person, a good worker, get married, have many children."

I replied in a sarcastic manner, "What if I never get married?"

"I'm certain your intended mate will come forth at the right time. It is meant to be, you will see," he replied.

She did enter into my life. My wife is a blessing and truly a gift from God.

I read Onasis' life, Nikos Kazantzakis and Elias Kazan all from Greek parents. They stated in their books the same challenge from their parents—'Then Xeris Yati Sis.'

At age forty, I read the in-depth reply—Kazantzakis' 'Return to Greco'. It took reading not only this book, but also all his books, to get answers. For example, in Zorba the Greek, Zorba asks the professor, "What's it all about?"

The professor replies, "We are amoebae feeding on a leaf. The leaf is the earth. The tree is the universe. All the amoebae are busy eating the leaf (earth). The lucky ones are those that lift their heads and look out at the immensity of it all and wonder."

Lesson # 28
General Mills

I cannot finish this book without relating one real ridiculous episode that happened.

I was in business for approximately nine months when receiving a phone call within my "out office" from the Vice President of Engineering of General Mills. He was interested in my pinch valve, stating it was ideal for handling flour and sugar. There were no pockets for food decay.

He stated, "I would like to come and visit you because we like your product."

By that time, my office had expanded a little, plywood being replaced by a cement block, two-person office. However, there still remained a dirt floor, old desk, typewriter, and four folding chairs. I had started construction of my cement block, 20 feet by 30 feet, (see photo page 30) "plant." It would be embarrassing to receive any client, much less a bigwig from General Mills. I, therefore, informed him I would be in Chicago, and it was a short trip from Chicago to Minneapolis.

"No, no. I'm going to the Food Show in New York with my Chief Draftsman. I will be flying in my company's jet so I will come to your office."

I shook a bit before I continued. "When you get to Pittsburgh, call me, and I will pick you up at the airport because the plant is located on a hilly, unpaved, dirt road, and may be difficult for you to find."

Ten days later, that appointment was confirmed.

I asked my wife to come to work and type some sort of fake letter.

"I can't come over there. You don't have any toilets!"

"Well then," I told her, "try to visualize what I go through on a daily basis, just picture my nine months of annihilation."

She said, "You really must need me," and agreed to come to work.

The road to my facilities was muddy and full of ruts. It was raining as we were waiting for the phone to ring.

Around 10:30 a.m. there was a knock on the door. Two immaculately dressed men complete with mud on their shoes, and the cuff of their pants came halfway into the door. It was the VP and his Draftsman.

I said, "You should have called me from the airport."

"Well, we thought since you were the President of the company, you would be busy. We hailed a cab, but it couldn't make it up this hill so we had to hoof it."

"Come in and sit down." I reached for the folding chairs. They stared at the dirt floor, and my wife, who was nervously typing a letter that said nothing.

We discussed features of the valve. They were both in agreement that it was a good valve for food service—no pocket for food decay—simple to operate.

"May we see your production facility?"

"Well, I just began building a cement block plant. No one is working right now; it is hunting season and the men are all off."

"We want to see it anyway."

At that moment, the rain had turned to a light snow, which was blowing through the plant (and I use the term "plant" loosely). There was some snow on the small junkyard lathe.

"Mr. Raftis, you have no glass in the windows."

I replied, "We Pennsylvanians are a hardy bunch." What could I say? That was the first thing that popped into my mind.

"Son, if you don't get some glass in these windows soon, you are going to freeze your ass off!" The VP almost cracked a smile. The draftsman chose to keep his mouth shut.

With that remark, I realized just how ridiculous this situation really was and began to stutter. "Let's g-g-g-go b-b-b-back to the of-f-f-fice." It was either nerves, or I was shivering from dampness and cold. Who knows?

Obviously, they had noticed the stupid set-up, but we talked about valves, but not for too long. They were chilled from head to toe, but at least had trench coats on for a little protection against the weather.

I started to stutter again, "L-l-l-ets g-g-g-get b-b-b-back to the airport." I just couldn't talk.

I drove them back to the airport, not much was said. To lighten the atmosphere, I did say, "I recently moved from another facility." Suddenly an ugly thought ran through my mind—they now must only imagine how decrepit the other facility must have been. My best bet at this time was to shut up the rest of the way to the airport.

The best mousetrap, they said. I had the kind of valve that would handle flour, sugar, and not plug with no pockets for food decay.

Talk about life's trying-not-ready-yet moments.

A small postscript at this point: They bought a few valves, but no matter how good the valve was for their particular needs, I was in no position to furnish them, and in the many sizes as they required, nor was I equipped to provide quantity. Much to my dismay, I knew I could never win over their confidence again.

Win some lose some.

That is not only in life, but that is also in business.

Lesson # 29
Tranquilizers

One day I went to work, and developed the shakes while drinking my coffee. I went straight to the doctor's office wherein he advised me that my blood pressure, pulse, and heart rate were all normal. Why do I have the shakes?"

"You're tense, worked up."

"I'm going to give you a prescription. Take these pills for one week. They will help calm you down."

"Are they tranquilizers?"

"No. Nothing but strong aspirin."

When I got home and showed them to my wife she advised me that they were indeed tranquilizers.

"That's it. I'm going to Puerto Rico for a week or two, and if I don't calm down, I'm selling the business. I'll be dammed if the business requires that I take these or any other pills in order to run it."

My wife was quite surprised with my reaction, and that I actually booked the ticket the next day to Puerto Rico for ten days.

Anastasia is a lovely, understanding wife, and at that time we had three growing children, but a very small insurance policy. My family would need food and shelter for at least the next twenty years.

I came to terms with myself in Puerto Rico s my thoughts became more relaxed and sincere.

My philosophy was, "If you can't handle the stress, get out."

I made a pact with myself—no tranquilizers—no narcotics— maybe a little booze. I chose to utilize my brainpower instead. After my two-week vacation, I returned relaxed, found direction, goals, and looked forward to the business's future with great expectations for not only myself, but family as well.

Tranquilizers are not the answer. I NEVER take them as they represent a false hope and only work temporarily. The problem you have has to be faced head on only one way, the RIGHT way. Cleanse your mind with thoughts of fixing what ever is wrong.

There are therapists you can speak with if necessary, but talk, cry, yell, scream, only do not take tranquilizers.

Business requires a brain running wide open at all times. Get a good night's rest. Do not let the business overpower the belief in yourself, have more than enough confidence so that whatever goes wrong <u>will</u> and <u>can</u> be fixed. When you think you're at the end of your rope, tie a knot at the end and hang on. Keep up your strength; take some time off to give yourself a new perspective and goal.

Stay cool and remember your health always comes first. Without it, you are unable to function properly much less run your own business.

If tranquilizers are needed—sell out—walk away. Your health comes first.

Lesson # 30
Goals and Cutting the Mustard

My particular goals in starting a business were:

1. To become independent.
2. To be awarded for the fruits of my abilities versus letting the boss get rich over the use of my brain, hard work, and ability.
3. Not getting fired after building up a territory.
4. To set a goal of $20,000 to $25,000 annual income (This was back in 1953.) Something attainable beats out the multi-millionaire-pipe dream.

Set reasonable goals that are attainable.
After you reach your goal and beyond, you need to set new goals, and be confident it can be done.

Confidence in one's self is definitely important.

NEW GOALS

Can I cut the mustard?

Sales to increase fifteen percent per year.

Money is not always the motivation, It is merely a fringe benefit.

Find out what motivation is best for you.

The challenge counts.

Can you cut the mustard? You bet!

PART III

THE VALUE

.

If the reader has come this far the "Reflections" that follow could be considered to be the real "jewel" section of the book. The purpose for making the journey, beginning when I was twenty-six, is clearly stated within "THE VALUE" pages. Building something—from an idea—to a dream—to reality is like heady wine, indeed. The exhilaration of accomplishment of goals remains fertile in my mind. The first sections entitled, "THE NEED" and "THE USE" described thoughts and feelings of my journey.

But the revelation of a legacy passed on to family lightens my step in my later years, fills my heart with joy, as my sons bring the RED VALVE COMPANY into the twenty-first century. I sleep well knowing the future bodes well for those associated with the company whether they are owners, employees, suppliers or customers.

Respectfully submitted,
Spiros G. Raftis

Author with wife

BETTER DAYS ARRIVED

George Raftis

102

Chris Raftis

Cynthia Raftis

Author standing next to 90" diameter storm water valve

Patents on display
Red Valve Co. Lobby

First Trade Show Exhibit
Also made in house of plywood

Left: Original Red Valve plant site in 1953, was an abandoned strip mine site.
Right: Red Valve Co. Rubber Manufacturing Plant in North Carolina

Reflection # 1
Family Succession

DO NOT REINVENT THE WHEEL.

The best way to start in this phase of your business "Family Succession Planning" is to go to the library or search through the Internet and get help early in this process.

Many Small Business Associations have seminars on "Family Succession."

In writing on this particular subject, the reader audience is so diverse as are the owners' personal needs that it is difficult to suggest a particular path.

Begin by reading and listening. I did with extreme absorption of every chapter read and every phrase spoken on the subject still imbedded in my mind.

First Basic Axiom—During the first year, eighty percent of all businesses fail. Of the survivors, twenty-five percent more fail within five years. The next failure is thirty-five years later when the founder runs out of steam.

This is definitely <u>not</u> the time (thirty-five years later) to begin teaching your sons and daughters how to run the business.

Second Basic Axiom—You cannot give advice from your grave nor can they be expected to ask questions from an Ouija Board or at a seance!

Statements proliferate, "Nobody can do it like Dad," and, "How about training us while you are alive, Dad?"

Most people I spoke with had problems with their dad letting go of the reins.

If your father is a doctor, chances are you will be guided in that direction, serving within the medical field.

I have married friends who are both lawyers. They have a daughter, who became a paralegal while the son was totally convinced (possibly brainwashed) that there was no other field available to him but law. Both children work within their family's firm.

Even when there is a professional Naval, Air Force, Army, Marine, and Coast Guard officer within the home, chances are one or more children in that family will choose the same branch of service, maybe even the same position. It's inevitable. Your surroundings help you choose in one direction, but you may turn your head towards another direction.

Not all offspring want to go into their parent's business and prefer taking their own time to find themselves, to discover what they want to do or become in life. Sometimes this process of finding oneself is overdone.

No matter what, it is important that the profession/business you are involved with be introduced to your children at an early age so they can become familiar with every aspect of the business, making their own decisions later on.

Keep in mind there are various consultants and firms who deal in family successions. I suggest that if you want to introduce your children to the family business at a much later stage in their lives with the hopes they can handle it, do so with great care.

Go to a consultant first, and then take your sons/daughters on the second visit. As an overview, I have seen better success using this method of help as opposed to contacting the consultant after you've proceeded to make a mess of everything.

Do not reinvent the wheel!

Reflection # 2
Is Your Succession Planning Easy

Winery businesses in Europe pass through not only one generation, but as many as four and five generations! Most of the time, their succession passes on to the eldest son.

This is old-world thinking, old-world family patience, and oldest son philosophy generally practiced within European and Middle East countries.

You live in America. The family wealth and business is generally divided more often among all the members of the family.

With some companies, the transition is simple. For others, it becomes traumatic in nature.

The easiest transition is for those who have just one heir. They are lucky.

A cop-out is to bring in an outside manager, particularly for the small business, not letting the sons/daughters run the company and grow with the business.

Reflection # 3
Siblings Day-to-Day Confrontations

Encouragement is the Name of the Game.

All young people need encouragement, enabling them to develop brainpower and management skills. Every progressive step each of my sons took received an avid "attaboy" from me. I looked for things to simply 'attaboy' them.

When my sons entered the business, I would compliment them in many ways. "You saved us money," "Great decision," "Liked your letter" "You handled that meeting like a pro," "Son, he thought he had you cornered," "I would have done it the same way."

If they asked about a problem, I would analyze the difficulty of the problem, and then, relate a solution letting them know that I was confronted with the same situation once.

Starting early with information before you run out of steam is the most fruitful approach. Day-to-day incidents, business confrontations, and money policies are a few of the many business problems.

Rather than solve problems alone, bring in a second-generation member, and have them listen and contribute advice or suggestions. Regarding compensation, establishing a salary base for owner and family members, and establishing incentive bonuses based on increase in sales or bottom-line-profits.

Explain the business is not a refrigerator meaning that every time hunger for more money, a new TV, or boat you cannot open the refrigerator door to satisfy this urge. It does not work. Take out only what one earns and is established as a salary. There must be money left in the business to pay the bills—supplies, wages, insurance, utilities, and unseen, unknown expenses.

Incentives create control. Teach this to your adult children.

When it comes to buying machinery, it should be discussed with sons/daughters. For example, a CNC machine can turn out a valve body completely machined in twenty minutes.

CNC machines cost $750,000.

Calculate hourly wages required turning out five hundred valve parts, add this to the vacation cost, holiday pay, workmen's compensation cost, company's share of social security payment, life insurance (even a $2,000 policy), and hospitalization costs.

Tell them no need to do an extensive feasibility study. This study in large corporations dictates CNC must operate a minimum of two shifts with consideration given for a 200% to pay back.

Family-owned businesses make a decision that afternoon, with the short cut, immediate, quick-cost calculations. You want to enjoy profitability and the sales advantage of faster production.

Inventory turnover is important.

NEW PRODUCTS—New products—another second-generation discussion. With large corporations, prototypes cannot be built before a market survey and feasibility study is made. This study can cost $25,000. They question if the new product works, what is the market?

Small family owned businesses can build prototypes of $2,000, test it and offer it to a few customers. Feasibility study money went into building a 'Rough' prototype.

We introduce at least one new product every year. New markets open up with new products and sales increase. Take-home pay from incentive plan increases.

Other straightforward answers to business problems come up every day.

The problems are most meaningful if they are part of a son/daughter's daily work-day and confrontation.

The problems do not have the same impact when reading about a situation.

You cannot give instructions from the grave so you'd better give them before that time comes.

Start early while you are still young, full of energy and have patience.

I personally know four owners of manufacturing businesses who never had their sons in the business.

"Why?" I asked.

"Because my son is just plain dumb!"

Another person answered, 'because my son just doesn't have what it takes.'

They all asked how I did it. My answer? It began many years ago with the "attaboys."

Actually, I don't see how anyone's child can be 'dumb' unless he happens to have a superhero type of father who performed brainwashing tactics on his own son, actually making him believe he is dumb! No "attaboys" here, just the usual father constantly nagging his son, making statements like, "What the hell is wrong with you?"

This is pure, unadulterated, verbal abuse by the parent. That child certainly knew he could never be as smart as his father. (Basically, he probably *was* a lot smarter, had he been given the chance to prove it).

If you have a problem reread Message # 5, "Fear of Failure" rename it. "I put the <u>fear</u> in my sons and daughters."

I wonder where the mothers are who are allowing this sort of thing to happen under the same roof? Many fathers, and mothers in some cases, are simply egotists—domineering people—not even realizing they have pushed their sons or daughters over the edge, placing them a state of mind considerably below average. Most of these adult children end up having no self-respect and generally can't stand their own lives, an attitude with no hope.

Watch your sons and daughters, let them take part in household events as well as in the family business. They need to feel participation, to feel needed, respected. They require your attention. When they have a question, answer it as best you can. Just let them participate someway in whatever the family has to offer.

I read another book—Domineering Father. It stated that a high percentage of leaders are "Domineering People." That's how they got there. It cautioned that switch must be turned off when you get home. Don't dominate your wife and kids.

I am glad I read this book. I decided I better "BACK OFF."

Reflection # 4
Decisions

One of the first of many business lessons I discussed with each son and daughter was related to making decisions.

I told them employees would come and ask them to make decisions within one week. Yes! One week!

Most employees do not want responsibility. Consequently, tell your offspring they, the employees, will push decisions on to them.

I gave my second-generation authority to make $1,000 decisions right away for the first three months.

I handed them also the following schedule:

After three months	$ 20,000 decisions
After one year	$ 50,000 decisions
After two years	$ 100,000 decisions
After three years	$ 500,000 decisions

After that, if you think your decision can bankrupt the company, talk to me or at least phone and discuss.

Other than getting them immediately involved in the business, you are also inferring to them they are smart enough to make decisions.

Reflection # 5
Parental Influence at Home

Everything on earth, everything in the cosmos, and everything astral seems to touch and affect you, serving to help you learn, grow, evolve, improve, and achieve your goals.

You cannot expect a child born in Calcutta, Bangladesh, or Sarajevo to have the same life as a child born to the Kennedy family, even if they are born within the exact precise moment in time. We are dealing with energies that flow and influence, not with the fixed and immutable.

Consider this aspect with your offspring...your daily routine, the casual conversations in your home. What influence do they have on your offspring? The experiences they've had listening to you talking about various subjects to others definitely influences their particular thoughts.

Certainly, compared with small talk in Calcutta and rural backward areas, there is no comparison.

Point out that if he or she wants to be self-employed, America is the land of opportunity. There are articles in local newspapers and magazines that write about self-made individuals. Cut these out and give them to your son(s)/daughter(s).

Single parents have an even greater task in building up their own self-confidence much less the self-confidence of their child, since they are usually already taxed to the limit with work and other obligations.

Take advantage and build on this!

Encourage your offspring. If you don't get him/her in the business, encourage his career be it teaching, hairdressing, pilot or airline stewardess, circus clown...whatever strikes his/her fancy.

Reflection # 6
Succession Planning—Why the High-Failure Rate?

I have to repeat the reason for high-failure rate of businesses after thirty-five years is lack of planning for the future. The founder of a business also, even at age sixty-five, is convinced nobody is as smart as he or can run the company as well, particularly an offspring or relative. I repeat, statistics state over eighty percent of ALL businesses fail the first year! Fifty percent of the survivors fail within five years. Thirty-five years later, the failure rate again zooms. Why?

Simply because the owner ran out of steam, joined country clubs, played golf, went swimming, took trips to Europe, and even got involved in politics. He found himself purchasing luxurious vehicles Mercedes, Jaguars, Chrysler LeBarons, or Cadillacs. Let's not forget the expensive Condo living! I plead guilty to all of the above.

The owner (father) says, "Well, I saw to it and hired a good manager." He forgot the manager was as old as he was and generally possessed an even less amount of steam and drive! The owner believes his son/daughter will eventually learn from the manager's instructions. Not so!

Most founders actually never take time to think this problem out. Therefore, there is no second generation coaching and the high-failure rate.

This is not what I did.

My sons and daughter got into the business; I wanted to ensure it longevity. I got them interested before I ran out of steam.

Reflection # 7
Silver Spoon In His Mouth

I read somewhere that it takes the founder a lifetime to hit one million dollars in sales, and the second-generation goes to twenty million easily.

My philosophy was let *them* build it up; let *them* take the pressures. Youth can handle it. The founder? He's liable to go die with a coronary!

I made sales calls with my sons. Spent time in the shop and office answering questions regarding product manufacturing, discussed improvements, innovations, and dealt together with them with banks, lawyers, CPAs, and customers.

My philosophy was that I wanted to enjoy what I had earned.

Let them all work for future growth! Do I still work? Of course! I get involved with projects I like. The ones I enjoy the most, developing new products.

I hold thirty-two patents. That keeps me out of their hair and the day-to-day problems of the company.

Occasionally the boys don't exactly like the way I run my projects, but I simply hang in there and listen to them. They have a chance to observe my fumbling and perhaps avoid doing the same thing when they reach my age!

I discussed with them the obstacles all second generations must deal with.

Son of Boss (SOB)? He has it made. First thing he has to psychologically fight are his peers. Fellow workers don't say too much, but they certainly do a lot of thinking!

"His sons sure have it made!"

Baloney is what I say!

Both sons bust their asses. They have more responsibility than a kid their age deserves. Dad says—go ahead, son. Keep up the good work. You can do it!

So tell your sons/daughters in the business:

> **Overlook the SOB title.**
> **You do it.**
> **You're good at it.**
> **I'm proud of you.**
> **You are really good!**
> **God Bless all of you for being here!**

Reflection # 8
Hey, George Made a Mistake

George made a somewhat serious mistake. He knew it—I knew it. I didn't cuss him out or call him a dummy. Mistakes, they occur almost everyday, in every place of business or at home. We all make them. I don't care who you are or what you do; you will make mistakes!

I said nothing that day or the next day. I didn't speak about it for three weeks.

After three weeks, I said, "By the way, do you remember such and such goof up three weeks ago?"

George replied, "I have been worried sick wondering when you would bring the subject up and yell at me."

"The easiest thing I could have done was to yell and curse when it happened and it would all be over with, right then and there."

"I guess that's right."

"This way you have been thinking about your mistake for three weeks and, hopefully, you have learned something and have also come to the conclusion that you lost our money, not my money. We should also discuss how to correct it. Remember, I made mistakes running the business.

No one yelled at me.

No one was looking over my shoulder.

I should extend to you the same courtesy."

Reflection # 9
Intimidation—Malaka

Do not intimidate your offspring.

Better to <u>light</u> a <u>candle</u> <u>than</u> <u>curse</u> the darkness.

When I was growing up in our parish, there were three altar boy buddies who had successful fathers, one father being an attorney. He made it because the ethnic trade trusted him. I don't believe he knew very much about law let alone encouraging his children.

Every time this attorney's son did something, his father called him a 'Malaka'. The Greek word Malaka translates into 'one who makes it soft'; in other words, he called his son a JAG OFF.

This boy was so intimidated that he was, is now, and always will be a failure, a Malaka. Never a word of encouragement from his father, i.e., 'You did good.' Even when he brought home an A on his report card, the old man's reproach would be 'Oh, so you finally got one. It's about time!'

The other altar boy's father had a restaurant. His old man stayed on his back like you wouldn't believe. He tolerated a steady diet of Malaka.

"Why can't you be smart like Spiros, the sexton's son." There was no end to the verbal mental beatings that boy had to take day in and day out.

Spiros works five hours, goes to school and receives A's. If he only knew how hard I had to work for a C!

His father had him working four hours a night in the restaurant.

This friend told me, "Listen, I live in a neighborhood where all the kids have money. I should be studying not jerking sodas! You, Spiros, work because you have to whereas I don't have to! I need the four hours to study. My old man is nothing but a tyrant. He hates my guts!"

Another failure! He could not run his father's restaurant even when he was forty years old.

The third altar boy had a dad who thought his son's middle name was Malaka. He dropped out of college in six months, put a brick through a department store window, and performed many similar acts, costing his father money. His father had him hospitalized when he smashed the window claiming he had a nervous breakdown to avoid jail.

Most successful people are domineering. That's how they got where they are in the first place. Unfortunately, they carry this attitude home with them. This attribute of dominance is normal and natural to them; they do not realize what tyrants they are. The wife and children definitely suffer under these conditions. An extremely dominating man generally takes it out not only on his child, but the wife as well.

I read a book about this subject, Effects of Domineering Parents.

Glad I did. I observed myself as being domineering. It helped me tone down. I started letting them come up for air!!

Back off, man...and dad, don't be a 'Malaka'!

Reflection # 10
Invite the Second Generation to Run Your Business

How do you get your children to get into the business?

It really begins with building up their self-confidence as they are growing up.

Ask them to give the family business a try. Tell them it's all going to be theirs eventually. Tell them to learn how to run it and make money for the rest of their lives.

Fortunately, my sons and daughter wanted to join the company. I guess because they heard mostly positive comments from me through the years about the business (or real bragging.)

They discovered later they could get a company car; they did not have to pay car insurance, gas, and other perks. They realized the perks afforded for being your own boss, and that more perks would be forthcoming. They liked this. Point this out.

Do whatever it may take!

Just remember however, entering your family business may be what YOU desire them to do, not necessarily what your sons/daughters really want. At least earnestly make the offer if they have not planned a specific career.

I thank God for my adult children.

They earnestly wanted to join the firm.

My business associates tell me, "Your two sons and daughter really love the business. They're dedicated, workaholics, positive thinkers - good marketing skills."

They are the reason our company has tripled sales since they joined the firm.

Reflection # 11
The SOBs (Sons of the Boss)

Youth Can Handle It:
My philosophy is 'let them take the pressures'. In all probability, youth can handle what the founder cannot.

My philosophy and yours should be enjoy what you've earned.

Start early in order that they have a chance to watch you fumbling your way through life and business. Perhaps they can avoid the same mistakes. Admit to your heirs that you've made a few mistakes during your lifetime.

"By the way, boys, me and your mother are fed up with this business. It's time to collect my salary and travel.

You grew up with small business problems and learned how to cope with all that stuff. They have serious big-business problems. Things have changed. Everything is different now.

Cut some slack!"

There definitely are bigger problems now such as more laws, Internet, higher insurance rates, fuel costs, postage rates, computer glitches. The next generation has weightier decisions. Train them at least with answers to the simple problems you had.

The person I feel sorry for is the SOB whose dad gave him the responsibility but not the confidence. Who tells him and continues to tell him everyday of his life, that he doesn't know what he's doing. What is tougher for a young SOB than to be called a dumb ass every day by his father, or even occasionally, while employees are thinking he has a big shiny silver spoon in his mouth!

It happens, so this is one reason, sons and daughters walk away from a business.

College does not offer courses "How to Raise Children 101" your on your own.

Reflection # 12
The Old Man's Idiot Mistakes

People, business associates say, "You have made it son! You inherited from your father a profitable business along with a legacy you must live up to!"

BULLSHIT!

He left stupid work policies, investment in some bad real estate, outdated inventory, bad leases, outdated equipment, useless inventory. I could go on and on. Dad, however, was Straight-Shooter Honest (just a little stupid).

I say BRAVO to the second generation that overcomes this inheritance ovation and must work in this current environment.

I told my friend that on my 50th anniversary, I thanked God I am living in America.

Thanked my dad for working hard, sacrificing many things, spending hours talking to me about what people are like—partners, etc. I attribute much of my success to his conversations, even though; my father did not have a business he knew human relations, and those were the best lessons I learned growing up.

I have a daughter, Cynthia. She took over my real estate holdings. I erected three new office buildings. She was so smart; she built the fourth at a smaller cost per square foot than my other buildings. Her building was smart.

You can do it, Cynthia! She did it.

I would be a failure in life if I merely enjoyed all the goodies in life, and didn't make an even greater effort to develop enthusiasm, management skills, challenges, and goals for my sons and daughter.

My father invested his labor, sacrifices and his entire life to make me who I am today. I therefore have an even bigger obligation to do the same for my sons and daughter.

Reflection # 13
"Dad, Let Go of the Reins!"

I joined a Family Succession Group.

There are many such organizations that are worth involvement. These seminars are free or have a minimal charge.

I served on a panel at one of these seminars. These group meetings are an exchange of thoughts on succession problems and solutions.

More participants complained in these sessions that their <u>fathers</u> <u>would</u> <u>not</u> <u>let</u> <u>go</u> of his control of the business. Sons/daughters work hard to help make it profitable, but dad <u>refuses</u> <u>to</u> <u>let</u> <u>go</u> of the reins.

I didn't have that problem because I trained my heirs to be much smarter than I, not to become Nerds!

One friend of mine told me his sons are so smart that they represent the only competitors in the world that could wipe him out. He didn't say that out of fear but rather for pride on the job he did in training those boys.

I know a man who owns a large string of fast food stores in Pittsburgh area. He refuses to give up the reins. When he goes to the Caribbean on vacation, he travels, phoning instructions at various intervals. There is no justification or trust here, particularly with his own flesh and blood, his sons.

When he dies, he definitely <u>cannot</u> <u>secure</u> a <u>phone</u> extension <u>from</u> his <u>grave</u> or use his cell phone. Cell phones are not developed that well yet.

Reflection # 14
Moral Support

Of all the previous advice, the most important statement to your son(s) or daughter(s) should be:

You are doing a great job!

This is why I am again discussing this very important area to build self-confidence in them.
You tell them:

You did a much better job than I could have.

Here are some of my lines for appreciation and support for my kids:

You bought castings cheaper, you sub-contracted to several machine shops to manufacture some of our parts cheaper!
You didn't sacrifice quality for savings!
You bought manufacturing equipment, and metal-fabricating equipment at attractive prices!
The air conditioner for the building is a superior design, and has lowered fuel costs.
George, Chris, and Cynthia did a better job than me!

I truly believe this.

SPIROS G. RAFTIS

Reflection # 15
More Than One Heir

The easiest scenario for Succession Planning is when you have only one heir.

Two or more heirs—*now here is a large can of worms!*

More than one heir—two sons—one daughter, any combination you need.

What's the problem? Why should the daughter have equal rights or any rights or shares?

The problem is that all men and women are NOT created equal!

Common Sibling Confrontation: "She's a girl, what does she know!" Even though, many women take over companies and are successful.

"I'm smarter than my brothers!"

You will hear comments such as, "...this one is too domineering," "...he is quicker at numbers, "...she can handle people better," or "...she is sarcastic." Each offspring with their own set of "missiles."

IT CAN AND DOES GET NASTY.

I met a girl at a Succession Seminar who said to me, "They are all bastards. I hate them, my father, the lawyers, and my own brother. They threw me out of the company for the stupid reason I am a girl and women don't need the money as much as a man with a family. That's why they threw me out! The succession attorney even supported their move to bring peace."

I met a man who threw his own wife out of a family succession plan, and she worked in the business. What a son of a bitch he was!

Many a company hire consultants who specialize in these conflicts.

The only good advice I heard was when confronted by a decision about sibling and you decide to turn over the keys and the running of the company, you should tell them:

"You're not getting this company for free. You must agree to accept this gift with the following commitment...that you will always work together as a team. Love one another!

Three sticks of wood can be broken easily individually, bind them together and they are tougher to break.

Appointing a board of directors may be the answer.

One man told me he had his sons and their cousins write a report on how they would run the company, what plans to build the company they visualized. It was obvious from the reports as to who was most qualified. The others reading his report accepted his appointment and future authority. This worked for them.

There are founders that appoint an outsider to run the business. In one case, the founder appointed an attorney with instructions to let two sons and daughter take over when they attorney felt they were qualified. Two of the sons have MBA in Business. Six years later, the attorney likes his salary and perks so he voices an opinion that they are not yet prepared to run the company. He won't even hire them for any position.

Another problem occurs when the father does not want to let go of the reins.

In the next section are guidelines and in the Appendix are organizations and firms that can and will help.

They will help siblings learn the importance of communicating as equals.

They will address the personnel issues of strategic and succession planning.

They will have siblings appreciate the differences in people and blend the strong points into a solid team.

PART IV

A CONSULTANTS BRIEF GUIDELINE ON SUCCESSION PLANNING

By

John Ward and Craig Aronoff

A CONSULTANTS BRIEF GUIDELINE ON SUCCESSION PLANNING

Succession is a lifelong process, not an event. Mr. Spiros Raftis understood this as he so eloquently told us throughout these sections; he wanted to have his family in his business, and he wanted to insure that he did not stay too long in control at the helm. The process of successful succession is more understood today than in the past, and best practices are presented at programs all over the world such as those at the Family Enterprise Center at the University of Pittsburgh.

John Ward and Craig Aronoff have long been thought of as the leaders in the family business field. As founders of the Family Business Consulting Group, they have consulted with many of the leading families around the globe as they move through the generations and have written many books on the subject. Once a founder understands that he has a family in business in his hands, he can start to plan what is next. Ward and Aronoff lay out their strategies for success in their series of books on the subject called Family Business Leadership Series. The steps to succession planning are as follows:

1. *Establish a Family Participation Policy.*
    Some families welcome all members into the firm; other families have policies that state entry is dependent upon jobs available that match member skills. Policies should outline spouse participation and rules for salaries, bonuses, and use of company assets such as planes, cars, memberships, etc. If you are planning to give stock to family members not in the business, develop governance models for passive shareholders, as they become a source of dissention if not given a voice or understanding of what is happening in the business.

2. *Provide Excellent Work Experiences to All Without Identifying Successor too Early.*
    Prepare family members for entering the business by assisting in the completion of their education and, if

possible, outside work experience. Oftentimes it is easier if the first boss is not dad or mom. Once they enter the firm, develop a job description with annual goals attached. Mentor the member as they learn all aspects of their job and provide positive encouragement, which cannot be overstated. It is critical to their sense of accomplishment, as well as their self-esteem.

3. *Commit to Family Business Continuity.*

Mr. Raftis made the decision early to keep the family in the business and not to bring in outside management. This is not always feasible due to age or preparation gaps. The most important criteria here is that the decision is made and communicated. This puts the family, employees, and other stakeholders on notice that this founder has a long-term perspective and is planning for another generation of the family to be in control. This also alleviates any game playing by the controlling generation that keeps everyone in the dark as to what's next or what the future holds. A family mission statement or creed is a good way to firmly let the world know your plans.

4. *Design a Leadership Development Plan.*

Every generation of a family business is unique and faces its own set of challenges. Sibling partnership stages tend to be more intense and volatile than any other. As a result of growing up in the same household, the level of intimacy and emotionality is higher. Siblings carry into the business all those memories and opinions of each other that they have held since childhood. Because each sibling may own a substantial minority in the company, a family business can be put in jeopardy when one sibling is angry, disenchanted, or unproductive and isn't functioning as part of the team. Siblings need to acknowledge that they hear, think, decide, and communicate differently. They also need to develop skills to deal with these differences— communication skills, listening skills, empathy, and appreciation for differences. They also need to develop policies for input and interaction with each other's spouses. This can be in the form of family meetings or family councils but should not be ignored. Pillow talk can be hurtful if not dealt with and understood up front. Plan for each of their roles and watch carefully as the leader skills emerge that the company will require taking it into the future. Then start to formulate your idea of your successor.

5. *Have an Active Board of Directors*

An active board of directors includes experienced non-family business leaders and individuals who are not tied financially to your firm such as your attorney or accountant. All corporate boards serve legal functions, approving changes to bylaws or articles of incorporation, approving mergers and acquisitions, declaring dividends, and so on. But generally, board functions derive from five key roles: ensuring effective governance; monitoring and improving business policy and strategy; providing advice and counsel to management; overseeing succession planning; and supporting family shareholders. If you are not ready for a full board, consider beginning with an advisory board or by adding several non-family members to your existing board.

6. *Clarify Business Strategic Plan*

Most entrepreneurs hate formal planning. They have built successful businesses without it. They favor action over talking. They live in the present convinced uncertainty makes it impossible to predict and plan for the future. Experience shows that planning is critical for long-term success in the family-held business that intends to remain that way. The business strategic plan and the family succession plan are interdependent and must move down a path in sync not in isolation. The process of planning forces owners, managers, and all members of the family to make timely decisions and also to keep their finger on the pulse of their family, business, and the global changes that surround us daily.

7. *Fund Parents Personal Financial Security*

Experience has shown that until the current generation feels that they are financially secure, it is difficult for them to transition out of the business. The business has provided them a lifestyle which they are comfortable in and that they intend to continue. They do not want to be held hostage by their children when it comes to their financial matters, and they are not going to be put into a situation where they have to ask for money. As with any retiree, they need to have their financial instruments in place that provide the income for their lifestyles and are not dependent upon the swings of the business.

8. *Identify Successors or Succession Selection Process*

While succession is a lifelong process, most of the work of preparing for the transfer of authority and control can be done in 5 to 15 years. Most owners begin thinking about succession in earnest at about 45-50 years of ages with plans to retire about 65. Typically, their children would be 25-30 with their formal education and outside work experience behind them. Beginning at this stage allows the 25 years needed to make a choice among multiple candidates. It allows time to develop and groom potential successors, to give them a chance to demonstrate their abilities and to pull together a family executive committee or family succession task force to help. By the time succession actually takes place, the process will be understood and the likelihood of conflict reduced. Once a successor has been chosen, five years is usually enough to permit training and testing of the heir apparent and to execute a smooth leadership transition.

9. *Complete Transfer of Ownership Control*

This last step is, of course, the most important and often the hardest to do. You have set the path, picked a successor, and now you must transition to the next part of your life. This is the time that you need to let your carefully chosen and prepared successor find their own managerial voice. You get to do all the things that you never had time for because of he demands of the family

FIVE SHEETS OF PLYWOOD:
A PRACTICAL GUIDE FOR STARTING YOUR OWN BUSINESS

business. Devoting time to activities that will be at least as creative and exciting as those you are leaving behind is critical to your satisfaction with the rest of your life. Your reward will be in setting back and watching your next generation taking your family business into the future and preparing it for transition to your grandchildren and great-grandchildren.

Excerpted from the Family Business Leadership Series by Craig E. Aronoff, PhD and John L. Ward, PhD. Visit www.efamilybusiness.com

RESOURCE LIST

PART V

START UP, ACCOUNTING and FINANCE GUIDE

By

Mr. Joe Myers

This is Heavy

Now that you are ready to take the chance of going into business for yourself, you face re-cutting time. You now have to deal with the business of the business. You now have to ask yourself how do I manage this creation, this idea. An entire industry has grown up on the very concept of business people not being able to manage their own business. This is the 'Management Consultant' industry. These people generally command high rates per hour to advise you on how to manage your business. Your accountant or lawyer may actually be filling this role for you.

This chapter is designated to present some basic start-up problems and ideas. This chapter explains the basic organizational structures available to you.

It is worth noting that before you decide on the type of enterprise you wish to operate, you need to understand your motivations in this whole process. For example, do you wish to pay as little tax as possible? Or are you looking to take your company public? This long-term outlook is important on how you organize and how to run your business. For example, it has been my experience that major corporations tend to be more concerned with increasing earnings, which improve the overall stock value of the company, while individuals and family owned businesses tend to be more motivated by tax saving.

As a start-up, you generally do not have any one with big earnings per share. But you do have to show your banker earnings. Therefore, at the start, you need capital and a paycheck; you do not need accolades. In other words, it's okay to show a loss 'if it makes sense tax wise'. Of course, you will need to explain your loss to the bank or other creditors, but that may be better than paying taxes with your much-needed capital!

First things first.

Provide for yourself.

Most consultants and bankers would suggest a financial plan. Banks like that sort of thing when you apply for a loan. You need to meet your plan, or the bank will lose confidence in your company, more on that later. So when you put the plan together, make sure you provide for yourself. Factor in a salary. You need to feed your family, and you need to live.

Factor in the taxes:

There are three or four basic forms of organizations; a sole proprietorship, a partnership and a corporation. Under current tax law, if you incorporated, you can be a "C" corporation or a Sub-Chapter "S" corporation. Of course, if you're in the clergy or a charitable organization, you can be a not-for-profit organization. This is a bit misunderstood; the name is not for profit, not non-profit. Just a quick note here, many not-for-profit organizations make huge profits, they just do not pay tax. Many of the executives take large salaries and are touted as fine upstanding citizens. Their organization simply does not pay tax; the Reverend Jesse Jackson comes to mind instantly. If your organization did not have to pay taxes, how large of a salary could or would you take? Of course the salary too is taxable, but think of how much more capital is available to pay salaries because you do not have to pay taxes. The top tax rate for individuals is 39.6% and is effective for taxable income in excess of $283,150 in 1999 and $288m350 in 2000 regardless of filing status. For married persons filing individually, then the top rate starts at $141,575 and $144,175 in 1999 and 200 respectively. The top tax rate for a corporation is 35% on taxable income over ten million dollars. Don't forget about the state; they also get a cut.

When choosing an operating structure, keep in mind the tax savings actually in the state taxes and not from the federal income tax. For example, in the state of Pennsylvania, the corporate tax rate is 10.5% while the individual rate is a flat 2.8%. In Pennsylvania it makes sense to be a Sub-Chapter "S" corporation to reduce the total tax rate to the individual shareholders. We will discuss the different organization, in a bit.

Let's talk a bit about the major failure for a business. The fatal error that small business people make, from which they rarely recover from, is not charging enough for their product or service. This tends to snowball into a financing problem because in order to make up for the poor pricing, they finance the business with the government's money. They do not either remit state sales tax or state and federal payroll taxes. I cannot over emphasize this enough.

The reality of the matter is simple when it comes to remittance of withholding taxes or sales taxes, "IT IS NOT YOUR MONEY!" Payroll taxes and the withholding is your employee S money, and the employer's portion is tax like any other tax, it has to be paid. In fact, this is your employees' money as well. The government simply has a duty to protect the rights of the citizens of the country, and they do it quite well.

They get real mad when you do not pay the tax. Not even bankruptcy can save you from paying the taxes. The officers' of the corporation cannot hide behind the corporate veil. The government will go after them individually. Sales taxes are the property of the state and now counties. They use this to fund schools and professional sports stadiums. They get upset if they do not get their money. They may work with you by letting you pay off the unpaid taxes as if it is a loan, but don't miss a payment. Not a good habit to get into of financing your business by using the government's money. Late penalty payments are steep as well. Not at loan-shark rates but steep, plus interest.

Simply, its not your money, collect it and send it to the government. Charge enough for your product and service, or do not get greedy (some people are not reputable and will steal these monies) if you expect to be in business for the long term.

This brings up the issue of over all finances. You need a plan. A simple plan, but a plan nonetheless.

YOU NEED SOME IDEA OF HOW FAR YOU CAN GO BEFORE YOU RUN OUT OF MONEY.

How much you may need to borrow at the bank or have available at the bank, such as a line of credit. Point to note, if you think you need $30,000, double it and get $60,000. There is always a pitfall you do not anticipate. If the bank won't finance you, then what's left? You could use credit card debt. This is tricky and requires a lot of careful monitoring. In this day and age of competition among banks for credit cards, you probably get three to four applications a week, at introductory offers. The nice thing about credit cards is that debt is unsecured. The bad thing about credit cards is that the interest rate is high and you eventually have to pay a great deal more.

Build a slush fund. The principals of wealth apply to every organization. You've got to have savings for a rainy day. Putting away ten percent or some amount of cash is a good idea. At first you will think how will I ever pay the bills, meet payroll, etc. This you plan for as well.

A plan, a financial plan. Keep it simple: list out the expenses you expect to incur, including your salary. List out the revenue you expect to generate. Subtract the two, this is expected net income. This is as simple as it gets. Do this for twelve, eighteen and twenty-four months. Adjust your plan as the facts and circumstances change, but keep the plan alive. Look for the downtrend, and adjust your business strategy. By the way, if you do not understand something, ask. Never be afraid to ask. If you do not understand your plan, do not execute it. This would be failure eminent. Only if you understand it can you manage and control it. Your professionals, lawyers, and accountants love extravagance in planning and ideas in research; they charge by the hour. They are the experts, but they can go over board with ideas and strategies which, on the surface, will make you a lot of money, save a lot of taxes, yet it never materializes. They will send you a nice letter, which you won't understand and probably won't implement. Keep things simple at first and second and third. It is the only way to keep control.

Manage your financial information, don't fear it. It usually is what it is. The accountants generally do not just make stuff up. They occasionally make mistakes; that's another reason to keep your finances simple and understandable so you can spot mistakes in the numbers before you make an ill-advised decision.

Determine early on in your business what they key indicators are. They are sometimes financial in nature and sometimes operational in nature. For example, inventory turnover, days outstanding to collect receivables, total orders booked in a day, total amount shipped, GROSS PROFIT MARGIN, number of inquiries, cash in the bank. Learn your indicators and keep a close eye on them.

Your employees: "here today, gone tomorrow".

In my opinion, there are two types of employees to hire—doers and thinkers.

I suggest that in the beginning you will need doers! The only person who has any vision and is capable of thought is you. You are hiring people to do things for you so you can go out and do the things that make money. Some of the tasks you need to accomplish are technical, such as accounting or engineering. Nonetheless, for the most part, they are repetitive tasks and need done every day. The fact that they are repetitive is evidenced by the fact that most accounting and engineering systems are computerized.

If you hire thinkers, be prepared to change your vision or change your employee.

Sole Proprietor—this is when you simply own the business. You file your taxes on Form 1040, Schedule C. You are entitled to all the expenses incurred to generate income like any of the other forms of organization. You pay tax on the net income at the individual tax rates. You are also subject to self-employment tax or social security if the net income of the business is greater than $400.00. That rate is 13.0% double the rate for an individual, but net the same taxes paid to the government if you were an employee with earned income. One half of the self-employment tax is deductible, just like the employer's portion of social security is deductible to the business. The advantage of this type of organization is that it is simple. There is no formal filing with the State to register the entity; the entity can cease just as easily as it started. The disadvantage is that all of your personal assets are at risk in the event of liability. You have no legal entity to hide behind. If you plan on being in business for along time this is not the entity to use.

Partnerships—this is a sole proprietorship for two or more people. However, administratively it is a little more complex. If you form a partnership, you will need to decide how the profit and loss is to be split between you and your partner(s), You can split the profit and loss any way you and your partners agree to do so, The partnership files a Partnership return. US Form 1065. No tax is due with the partnership return; this is what the professionals refer to as an information return. Your share of the profit or loss is reported to you on a form called a K-1. Every partner receives a K-1. The government receives a K-1. This form is in essence the W-2 for the partners. The partners report the income or loss on their individual tax returns and pay tax on the income at their individual tax rate. These is interesting in that the partners could all be in different marginal tax brackets and, therefore, pay more or less taxes than their partners. The accountants like this because it presents opportunities to minimize taxes by shifting income. However, better to get the income and pay the tax. Now keep in mind that just because there is income does not necessarily mean there is any cash. The cash could be tied up in accounts receivable or inventory or in notes receivable that one of your partners has. Remember income does not always produce cash, more on this subject later.

The legality of a partnership in its base form makes every partner liable for every action of every partner. One partner's actions can put every partners' personal asset at risk to cover the liabilities for the partnership. Before you form this type organization, you better be sure of whom you're in business with. One partner stiffing another partner is not uncommon. Even the accounting firms were at risk at one time from this type of entity. This is why I suppose they are picky about who becomes a partner. However, with everything else the system tries to make things equitable, so LIMITED PARTNERSHIPS and LIMIT LIABILITY CORPORATIONS were written into the law. Both of these entities operate essentially the same as a partnership but attempt to limit the liability of each partner shareholder to their interest/investment in the company and company's assets. There are no formal fittings with the state to form most partnerships.

Every time a partner leaves for whatever reason, including death, technically the partnership ceases and a new one is formed. Liquidation of a partnership is tricky because of the basis each partner has. This is strictly a tax concept to determine gain or loss and also the deductibility of losses. Basis essentially is what you put into the business plus profits, less withdraws, less losses. This is akin to your cost in a stock.

If you decide to form a partnership get a formal partnership agreement. This is a document that explains the division of the partnership, establishes the partnership, and explains the reason and purpose of the partnership. This document explains the deal in the event there is ever a misunderstanding of the original agreement. Formalizing agreements is never a bad thing. If your business associate does not want to put your agreement into writing, run as fast as you can because a big mean dog is chasing you and you will get bit.

The final major entity is a Corporation. A corporation is like a partnership and is a separate legal entity. Shareholders or stockholders own a corporation. When you form a corporation as a business you are not only a stockholder, but if you work in the business, you are also an employee like every other employee. Well not like every other employee because I am sure you will take full advantage of your ownership and vote yourself to the presidency of the corporation. You must chair the board of directors. And since you make all the decisions, you are probably the chief operating officer. And since you will make the financial decisions, you may as well be the chief financial officer as well. Someone has to control this unruly bunch of executives, so as a shareholder and director, you better hire a Chief Executive Officer. Probably someone you can trust, someone with your vision and foresight, someone you can communicate with quickly and will follow the board's direction, someone like you.

You see a corporation can be more complex. First you have to register with the state. You have to have a charter, a set of by-laws to govern the operation, a slate of officers to run the corporation, and meetings to discuss the course the corporation is on. These minutes of the meeting need to be recorded for all concerned to review. Interesting that on an IRS audit, one of the first things the IRS asks for in a corporation is the minutes of its meetings, board of directors, shareholders, and any special purpose meetings held. Much is documented in the minutes, much are not. In a small start-up company, it is a good habit to have minutes. It shows that there is the form of the corporation. The IRS likes that. They think you are playing the game properly.

Taxes: A Corporation is a separate legal entity and required to pay taxes. The low-end bracket is 15%. This does not receive much press because there is no glamour in reporting small company income. This bracket is from $0 to $25,000. From a planning standpoint, if you have a lot of other income, which pushes your personal income into a higher bracket, and you start a business, which generates income, by not incorporating, you may be paying more taxes on the business profits than necessary. Every situation is different, but do not just set up an entity without knowing all the exposures. Of course the government wanted to give the little guy a break, so they created the Sub Chapter S corporation concept. This, in simple terms, is a corporation that receives all the legal benefits of being a corporation. That is, limited liability but is taxed like a partnership. That is, the income is passed through to the shareholders in proportion to their ownership and reported on their personal income tax returns. Not all states recognize S-corporations for all industries, so it gets a little bit complex. Beyond the scope here. The key is that you get the benefit of corporation legal protection and taxed at the individual rate. But you will remember this may not be a big deal since the federal individual rates are actually higher in top brackets than the corporate rates. But do not forget about the states. They often cause a situation where the combined federal and state rate is lower than the combined corporate federal and state rate. So you've got to plan a little and understand your situation.

It is not likely that you will be involved in a professional corporation so I am not going to discuss it at this point.

Limited partnerships are typically associated with real estate investing and syndication. The way they work is that a general partner is established who acts as the manager. The limited partners are generally investors. The concept of a limited partner is that the partner's liability is limited to his investment and the assets of the partnership.

Budgeting.

As I mentioned earlier, you need a budget. Now do not misunderstand that this has to be a complicated process. A budget is a guide. It is a living document and can really help the ship when things get off course.

The underlying principal of a budget is to list out everything you know about the business you are getting into. Most businesses fail because of financial reasons in the first year. In fact, I believe in this process for all encounters where money has the potential of being a central issue. In fact most marriages fall apart over money or lack of it. This only makes because psychologically, women are more concerned than men, while men are more concerned about new toys. The two can clash, particularly when the two cross.

So after you've listed all of your assumptions about your business, which includes how much you're going to make in total or gross revenue. This goes at the top of the page. Next start listing out the expense items. These are salaries, rent, utilities, cost of materials or products you are going to sell, office supplies, and so one. The difference between the gross revenue and the expenses is the net income. Expenditures such as equipment are capital in nature. That means it is going to last more than a year. These are not expenses, but rather they are assets. They are recorded on the balance sheet. The balance sheet is a listing of what you own and what you owe. The difference is what you are worth, called net worth, or net equity. Net worth is the measure of true wealth. Positive net worth is good, negative net worth is bad.

The equipment you purchased and recorded as an asset is presumed to have a useful life. As such, you should reduce the value of the equipment over its useful life. This is known as depreciation and will ultimately become an expense of the business. No free rides. Everything becomes an expense. However, how much to depreciate every year has been a subject of accountant's debates for years. The accountants have developed many methods to calculate the amount of depreciation expense. In the old days this was an area of much disagreement with the IRS. You see the more depreciation expense in a year the lower the income. So in 1980, the federal government statutorily determined useful lives of assets and the method to use. Since 1980, Congress has changed the system several times in an attempt to raise taxes. The most notable are the changes to real estate, which has gone from depreciation over twenty years to thirty years to 18.5 years to 39.5 years. Why a half a year? Who knows but it must have generated enough tax revenue to keep the life from being forty years, but not enough to be thirty-none years. It also gives the accounts an additional calculation to make.

CONCLUSION:

In starting a business, there is no single bit of advice that will assure you of success. As you have read in these many sections, there are many challenges, obstacles, and unexpected confrontations. Hopefully, this practical guide will help you overcome a few of them.

As I look back at my lifetime endeavors, all I can truly conclude is—

Only in America and God Bless America!

I have met many retired entrepreneurs while in Florida in my winter residence. These are Americans and immigrants who made it from scratch in diverse types of businesses. They struggled and sacrificed. Universally, they *all* say *God Bless America!*

They are the majority. People that inherited wealth are in the minority.

In England, France, India, Japan and Greece, the struggle is many times more difficult, almost next to impossible. Bureaucracy stymies their growth. Americans are the most innovative people on earth! Americans look for and want improvements. Their success is attributed also to the fact that they bring a product to market one or two years earlier than competitors overseas, excelling in marketing.

My company, for example, can attribute its ongoing growth, not only to new product development, but also to an ongoing marketing ability.

If you can't afford a large budget immediately for marketing and advertising, do this as soon as possible.

Also develop the ability to *PULL YOURSELF OUT OF THE BUSINESS* and look at it objectively. Where are you going? Is it smart? Is it stupid? Does this new agreement or commitment represent a good investment or jeopardize you? Can you lose it all?

My company, for example, replies, "No Quote" if the job is really large, and profit margin low.

Be a practical person. Join trade organizations because people help each other.

Don't reinvent the wheel.

Clarity of thought—right decisions will make you successful and rich.

My hours were 6:00 a.m. to 5:00 p.m. Monday through Friday, half day on Saturday. That drained me enough. I had a life to live, a wife and children, the new motion of 'Quality Time!'

Keep your heirs in mind. Don't be so wrapped up in one thing or another and neglect encouragement to them. Make "attaboy" or "attagirl" part of your vocabulary. They are automatically looking up to you for advice and information.

Don't forget to ease off. Stop to smell the roses.

Getting them in your business has many benefits. You will run out of steam. Spend some of the 'gold' you've made for yourself. Enjoy your life!

Your children may be smarter than you, as in my case. They grew up with a computer on their lap!

Almost anything can be figured out with the expertise of computer Internet connections. Give them credit.

Good luck—make every decision with care and knowledge. Pray for the clarity of thought. You, too, can be a success!

APPENDIX

WEBSITE & RESOURCE LIST FOR FAMILY SUCCESSION PLANNING:

1. FAMILY BUSINESS CONSULTING GROUP

   In addition to the Family Business Leadership Series, discussed above, there are numerous other books as well as a monthly newsletter on breaking topics of interest. Leading speakers are available to your organization on family business issues as well as private consultant. Visit www.efamilybusiness.com or call 1-800-551-0633

2. **FAMILY FILM INSTITUTE**

   Numerous books and articles are available as well as listing of all university-based educational program and seminars. Visit www.ffil.org

3. **CENTER FOR CREATIVE LEADERSHIP**

   Offers a wide range of training programs, seminars and workshops at four locations nationwide. Areas include leadership and management development affecting change, creativity, and organizational skills, working with others, and promoting teamwork. Visit www.ccl.org or call 919-545-2810

OTHER RESOURCE LIST

UNIVERSITY OF PITTSBURGH

The family Enterprise Center at the University of Pittsburgh Katz Graduate School of Business provides educational programs for the family in business. Other activities include assistance with formulating Board of Directors and peer advisory groups. Call Mrs. Ann Dugan 412-648-1544, University of Pittsburgh, First Floor, Posver Hall, Pittsburgh, PA 15260 for details.

Mr. Craig E. Aronoff, PhD
The Family Business Consulting Group
1220-B Kennestone Circle
Marietta, GA 30061

Mr. John Ward, PhD
1111 Forest Avenue
Evanston, IL 60202

Mr. Jim Kwaiser, Challenges, Inc.
911 Aztec Train
Mercer, PA 16137
Telephone: 1-800-273-8307

Mr. Robert Williams, Esq.
William Coulson
15th Floor. 1500 Two Chatham Center
Pittsburgh, PA 15219
Telephone: 412-454-0222

* * *

ABOUT THE AUTHOR

I, Spiros G. Raftis, at age 26, started a manufacturing business. I had no business plan, no real product, and, more importantly, very little money—because I was fired. I was devastated. I had devoted maximum effort, abilities, and long hours as a salesman for the owners of the company; in fact, I bought shares.

My decision to start my own business was to—
PREVENT GETTING RIPPED OFF AGAIN.
I was convinced—

OWNING YOUR OWN BUSINESS AFFORDS THE ONLY OPPORTUNITY OF BEING DIRECTLY AWARDED THE MAXIMUM RETURN ON ONE'S ABILITY.

I did not write this book to make money; I want to share practical advice with anyone starting a contemporary business. This is a no-nonsense book with non-MBA-theories. Most of the messages, lessons, and reflections within are my experiences. Perhaps, to some, these confrontations would not be extraordinary. I did not anticipate any of these events, but I know now going into business everyone will have to face what is written in these pages.

For example, I thought after one year in business getting a loan from a bank would be easy. Instead, I got a lesson from my banker. I still remember his words, "Spiros, if something happens to you how does the bank get back the money it loaned for your valve business? The bank does not want to run a valve company."

The pages repeat ideas that have been proven to be valuable for anyone seeking success in starting a business. It is a <u>must</u> <u>read</u> <u>must</u> <u>buy</u> book.

* * *

Spiros G. Raftis was born and raised in Pittsburgh, Pennsylvania. He graduated from the University of Pittsburgh in Metallurgical Engineering.

Spiros married Anastasia, and they have two sons, George, Chris and daughter, Cynthia. All are involved in the Red Valve Company, Carnegie, Pennsylvania. His current endeavor is designing new style valves for environmental applications.

* * *

As an overview, or as I look back, I have come to realize that my biggest assets were my self-confidence and determination.

You will need both of these to succeed.

Spiros G. Raftis

CPSIA information can be obtained at www.ICGtesting.com
Printed in the USA
LVOW060316171012

303180LV00003B/19/A